# History of Costume

# History of Costume

4   BC – AD 1500

Illustrated by Faith Jaques with a commentary by Margaret Stavridi

Publishers   PLAYS, INC.   Boston

First American edition
published by Plays, Inc. 1970
Library of Congress Catalog
Card No. 68-8264
I.S.B.N.0-8238-0079-2

First published in 1970 by
Hugh Evelyn Limited
9 Fitzroy Square, London W1
© 1970 Hugh Evelyn Limited

Printed in Great Britain by
Davenport Askew and Company Limited

*music*

*mux*

## List of Colour Plates

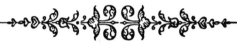

# Sources of Reference for the Plates

PLATE 1

a, b. Vase paintings. *c.* 570 BC. Florence, Museo Archeologico.
c. Vase painting. *c.* 445–50 BC. Paris, Louvre.
d. Vase painting. *c.* 460 BC. Paris, Louvre.
Alabastron and cup from Paris, Louvre.


PLATE 2

All frescoes.
a, d. Cerveteri frieze. 6th century BC. Paris, Louvre.
b. Tomb of the Augurs. *c.* 530 BC. Tarquinia.
c. Tomb of the Leopards. *c.* 500 BC. Tarquinia.


PLATE 3

a, b, c. Bas-relief. 1st century AD. Rome.
d, e, f. Ivory diptych. AD 395. Monza.


PLATE 4

All mosaics.
a, b, c. Ravenna, San Appollinare Nuovo. 6th century.
d. Ravenna, San Vitale. *c.* 550.


PLATE 5

a. MS. Bible of Charles the Bald. 9th century. Paris, Bibliothèque Nationale.
b. MS. Otto III, Reichenau Gospels. *c.* 1000. Munich, State Library.
c. German MS. 1080–1150. Salzburg, St. Peter's Monastery Library.


PLATE 6

a. MS. Siegburg Lectionary. 1175–1200. London, British Museum.
b. English MS. Cotton (Nero C.4). 1150. London, British Museum.
c. Hebrew MS. 1275–1300. London, British Museum.
Seat from MS., 1175–1200, British Museum. Lectern and desk from MS., 1050–1100, British Museum.


PLATE 7

All from German MS. *Die Minnesinger.* *c.* 1325. Heidelberg University Library.


PLATE 8

All from English MS. *Luttrell Psalter.* *c.* 1340. London, British Museum.


PLATE 9

All from frescoes by Simone Martini. *c.* 1325–35. Florence, Church of S. Maria Novella.


PLATE 10

All from English MS. *Luttrell Psalter.* *c.* 1340. London, British Museum.


PLATE 11

All from French MS. *The Book of Hours of the Duc de Berry.* *c.* 1415. Chantilly, Condé Museum.


PLATE 12

a, d. School of Jan van Eyck: *Hunting Party at the Court of Burgundy.* *c.* 1430. Versailles.
b, c. Jan van Eyck: *The Arnolfini Marriage.* 1434. London, National Gallery.


PLATE 13

a. Bayeux tapestry. *c.* 1070.
b. English MS. *c.* 1295. Oxford, Bodleian Library.
c. Andrea del Castagno: *Farinata degli Uberti.* 1445–50. Florence, Convent of S. Apollonia.
d. Giorgione: *Italian Knight.* 1490. London, National Gallery.


PLATE 14

a. Fresco by di Bartolo. *c.* 1440. Siena.
b. Pisanello. *c.* 1440–50. Chantilly Museum.
c. Flemish MS. *c.* 1480. Paris.


PLATE 15

All from Flemish MS. 1460. Holkham Hall.


PLATE 16

a. Hardwick hunting tapestry. Flemish. *c.* 1450. London, Victoria & Albert Museum.
b, c. Flemish tapestry. 1450–75. New York, Metropolitan Museum.
d. Flemish MS. *Roman de la Rose.* *c.* 1490. London, British Museum.

PLATE 17

All from Flemish MS., *Chronique d'Angleterre*, by Jean de
Wavrin. 1480. London, British Museum.


PLATE 18

a.  Pinturicchio: *Return of Ulysses*. 1500. London, National
    Gallery.
b.  C. Crivelli: *Saint Roch*. *c*. 1480. London, Wallace
    Collection.
c.  Fresco by Mantegna. 1465–70. Mantua, Castello di
    Corte.
d.  Fresco by Francesco Cossa. *c*. 1470. Ferrara, Palazzo
    Schifanoia. Cat from a.


PLATE 19

a, c.  Carpaccio: *Legend of St. Ursula*. 1490–95. Venice,
       Academy of Fine Arts.
b, d.  Fresco by Ghirlandaio. 1490. Florence, S. Maria
       Novella.


PLATE 20

All from Flemish MS. *Roman de la Rose*. *c*. 1490. London,
British Museum.

# Preface

While costume historians offer an ingenious series of reasons for man's adoption of clothing – protection, modesty or sexual display – one fact stands out clearly, that he has rarely studied the lilies of the field since he started to cover himself with skins or dangle a string of shells or beads on the most suggestive part of his anatomy. It seems obvious that northern Paleolithic men made body coverings out of the only material available, the skins of the beasts they had killed for food, for the same reason that they huddled round fires in caves – to keep out the rigours of the Ice Age. Their contemporaries in southern climes with no such compelling necessity could concentrate on the display impulse by variations in the design and placing of the shells or beads. Although no Stone Age suiting has been preserved for us, the delicately carved and eyed needles of the Magdalenian period, up to 17,000 years ago, would hardly have been made without the purpose of sewing skins together. Ideas came few and far between in the painful establishment of civilisation and it was many a long year before the possibility of making material dawned on the mind of Neolithic man – or woman, as it was most likely she, when doing her domestic chores, who realized that large pieces of material could be made in the same way as she had plaited grass or vine stems to make baskets or mats. Another step forward came after the domestication of sheep when it was found that the natural wool made a soft, springy thread if pulled out and rolled continuously while feeding in more loose pieces of the fleece. From then on ideas flowed and with an object to inspire him man began to practise the wonderful craft of textile-making by working out patterns in the texture, pieces of which have been found at the Neolithic lake-side sites in Switzerland. It was then that the potentialities of dress must have struck the more enterprising leaders of clans or tribes as signifying a distinction of rank or wealth. Head-dresses were undoubtedly the earliest form of real adornment. A tall crown, or hat, would add majesty to an already commanding figure (and did lots for an insignificant one) while the effect of a drape or train does not seem to have long escaped the notice of the leaders of men. In this way

fashion began, and has remained a mirror of man's thoughts and personality at any point in history. Fashion has never merely 'come about'; its changes have followed the inspiration or whim of some exhibitionist individual or have been the outward manifestation of group philosophy. Somebody first thought out and fashioned a pair of trousers against the cold; someone first flaunted a crinoline-frame for reasons best known to herself and somebody, responding to the trend of a permissive society, gave the signal for jeans and the mini skirt.

Climate has not been the main factor in controlling regional differences in clothes, since some of the brighter dwellers in hot climates discovered that clothes insulated against great heat and have long been seen muffled up in the hottest parts of the earth. The raw material for making thread played the greatest part in distinguishing differences of appearance. The dwellers by the great rivers found that the flax growing there made a fine strong thread; the nomad farmers used the wool from their sheep or goats; the cotton trees and shrubs were most obliging and the Chinese encouraged the output of the silkworm. The pre-historians and archaeologists are pushing the period of man's domestic achievements so far back in time that we cannot say for certain when civilisation first graced the scene in hand-made clothes. We do know that the Egyptian looked distinctive and cool in his flax-woven muslin and the people of the Middle East really stylish in fringed and ornamented woollen garments in the fourth millenium BC. Their jewellery and head-dresses had reached a peak of sophistication in design and craftsmanship that speaks of a long previous practice in the handling of material. The unwise virgin who had had no time to finish her hair-do when she followed Queen Shubad into her tomb and the Valley of Death at Ur, had rolled up her woven silver hair-ribbon in her pocket where it was found by her side 4,725 years later. The people of the West were not so highly developed sartorially at this period; their garments of a much later date, which we see miraculously preserved from peat bogs of Scandinavia, tend to be utilitarian rather than stylish, in woven or knitted wool, though their metal-work and jewellery would be thought very suitable wear at the present day.

For the purposes of this History, which deals only with the costume of Europe, we propose to ignore the sporting, chariot-driving Mycenaean barons of Bronze Age Greece (who, it will be further explained, had, from scant evidence, a very exotic and Middle Eastern air and disappeared into the mists of pre-historic myth) and take Greece of the early Iron Age as our prototype House of Dior. The real fashion creators were the new invaders, the mysterious Dorians who used the wool of their sheep to fashion rectangular pieces of material with which to drape themselves in a characteristic style which we see first, very dimly, on geometric vases then, decoratively, on black figured vases and finally in the familiar and graceful lines of the Classic style. Rome adopted this costume either from the early Greek colonies in Italy or in a roundabout way from the Etruscans who were looking very Greek when they laid the foundations of Rome. Roman contact with the barbarian North and final overthrow by its warrior tribes fused the two cultures, and the newcomers' important and comfortable item of clothing – trousers or leg covering – was added to the tunics and drapes of Classic dress and became standard fashion for many centuries. The Christian Church was responsible, with its emphasis on the errors of worldly vanity, for the relatively unchanging character of costume until the end of the first millenium as, from the time of Constantine, its tenets ruled the spirit and behaviour of man in every detail. Byzantine dress added a little grandeur to the scene but only in exotic material and ornament. The art of the Eastern Empire had become too hidebound and stylised to change in style. Charlemagne, around AD 800, may be said to have dropped the first stone into the stagnant pool of European culture, starting the ripples which were to have such an effect on man's social life in later centuries. The new approach to learning started men reasoning and questioning their role on earth, in direct contrast to the Church which took a dim view of any independent thinking or human philosophy. Charle-

magne's attitude, however, cannot be said to have caused any rapid changes in men's appearance as the great ruler does not appear to have had any personal interest in clothes.

Fashion is one of the refinements and fripperies of life. The spice of vanity, leisure and an audience are necessary for costume to assume an importance in civilisation. A more congenial atmosphere arose when the barbarian barons had settled down in their various parts of conquered Europe and become princelings. It was not until the fear of imminent judgment and damnation had faintly receded and an urban life, with a mixed society of court, merchant class and peasants had been established, that fashion could flourish.

It is first noticeable in the courts of Provence where apparently the Knights had the time to loll about, compose poetry and entertain each other in the intervals of energetic combat. The whole peculiar cult was called 'chivalry', and the new accent on sensual love and the competition in the fields of popularity and combat certainly put a polish on the manners of society and brought out the first exaggerated lines and details of costume. Due to the change in shape of armour, clothes became tighter and men's tunics, with the new interest in the shape of the body, crept up the thigh to show long and often parti-coloured legs, while sleeves widened and gowns trailed. The Burgundians then became influential, blossoming forth with some really showy personalities who, backed by the skill of their craftsmen, made dazzling figures in the fierce competition for power with France, resulting in some fantastic creations in clothes with mantling like many-feathered birds on head-dresses, sleeves and hems, all accompanied by the tinkling of hundreds of little bells. The Crusades had had a hand in drastically changing the picture of the Middle Ages. If nothing made allies loathe one another quite so much as these early package tours, they did get people on the move and if their members were lucky enough to come back with their lives the West was livened up with exotic ideas and souvenirs from the more cultured East. One item was the design of the pointed Arab arch, and its concept, when introduced into European architecture, suggested exciting parallels in art and dress. As Gothic cathedrals grew tall and narrow on forests of ribbed vaulting and buttresses flew and thrust upwards, man made himself as nearly a replica of a piece of architectural detail as possible without encasing himself in plaster. Hats and head-dresses shot up into points, bodices tightened and tunics narrowed into rigid pleats while the toes of shoes were pulled out into long, inconvenient rigid points which exactly echoed the narrow-minded behaviour of the wearers.

The settling-down process and new learning which had produced the Troubadours in Provence and the Age of Chivalry had quite a different effect in Italy. The great Humanists, responding to Nature, preached the doctrine of the fulfilment and enjoyment of life and of man taking responsibility for his own soul. Though their ideals grew a bit addled in practice, they awoke man to an awareness of nature and a sense of pleasure in his surroundings resulting in an upsurging movement in scientific curiosity, literature and art. Some of the Italian principalities and dukedoms went so far as to practise the ideas of liberal government and the general atmosphere grew more expansive all round – an effect we can judge for ourselves in the manner and dress of the gracious people in Renaissance paintings. Even the pleats and tatters of the Gothic fantasies look rounded and comely in paintings by Pisanello, and the elongated and angular extravagances of the northern fashion simply do not appear in the vast pictorial record of the Italian people of the fifteenth century.

Italy had been fortunate in being settled by the Lombards, the only barbarian tribe with any claim to an artistic heritage which, mingled with the latent indigenous talent, brought out the astonishing phenomenon of Renaissance art. The creation of beautiful luxury goods soon led to a heavy demand from less skilled nations with a resulting increase in the standard of living of the craftsmen and the fortunes of the merchants.

In the north the rich merchant class had risen from the people, through joint activities in the Hanseatic League; in Italy the leading, ruling families were the patrons and distributors. They had done very well for themselves, as war profiteers, by hiring out their fleets as transports for the Crusades and they continued to do so in times of peace as general merchants for luxury goods from the East and all the glorious products of Renaissance Italy. In all this commerce on the grand scale, England actually established herself as a member of an early European Common Market with her exports of wool and top-grade cloth, and even maintained a foothold in Flanders as a clearing-house for her goods. Appreciation of all things Italian gradually transformed the shape of clothes in the rest of Europe. Although eventually overwhelmed by its envious neighbours the influence had already been passed on when, in the 1480s, France, Burgundy and Germany began to ape the open-shirted, wider silhouette of the Venetians and Florentines.

It was now generally recognised that appearance became of great importance in the competition between all the nations elbowing for prestige and power in Europe, and fashion began to change more rapidly as the demand for new ideas grew, communication through exploration and the new art of printing developed and the competitors exchanged the lead. By the end of the fifteenth century people were beginning to want to look like the most successful of their fellows and a more universal style became apparent when the Austrian Hapsburgs began to dominate Europe and the centre of influence in fashion moved northward once again.

The aim of this History being to trace the influences that affected the main stream of fashion, Spanish and eastern European styles in the Middle Ages have not been discussed, as for the most part, these countries followed the fashions of their neighbours and contributed very little to the general evolution of costume until the sixteenth century.

PLATE I

# *The Greeks* BC

We are not at all sure when the people of Europe started wearing hand-made clothes instead of skins. The development of crafts such as pottery and weaving can only happen when the basic economy of providing enough food for the population is no longer a daily anxiety and is in the hands of one section of the community leaving the craftsmen to concentrate on their art. It was the introduction of the metal industry of the invading tribes that raised the standard of living sufficiently for people to start worrying about the cut of their clothes. Central Europe has always been the melting-pot of races and it was here that metallurgy developed and trade commenced promoting the diffusion of ideas even though it was a painful process. History *will* go on repeating itself and our modern distrust of a totalitarian system may spring from a built-in, deep-in-the-unconscious fear of the upsetting hordes who, through the ages, have borne down on Europe with battle-axes, bronze chariots and nasty iron slashing-swords in successive waves from the steppes of Russia. They came first for land, then for minerals, and finding both they settled among the previous farming communities and added their mite of culture to the common stock. The bronze-working warriors who stayed in the north gave it its forge-like Wagnerian image with the clash of hammer on anvil and the glow of fire and running metal. They may have known the art of weaving, as one of their divinities, rejoicing in the name of Frigg, had a distaff as her symbol, but such a domestic deity was hardly in keeping with their battling pantheon and was most likely an adoption from the gods of the more docile farming community with whom they settled. The clothing of these northern people was strictly utilitarian, even after many centuries: a one-piece shift for women and a shirt and baggy leg-covering for the men (which, incidentally, did come in useful for later Europeans) but they really let themselves go in the design of armour and metal ornaments, which had long and widespread repercussions.

Demeter is said to have first divulged the secret of cultivation to the Greeks; it would be interesting to know from where they got their genius for fashion design, for it was they who first put style into mere body-covering in Europe. Around 1600 BC Greece was invaded by a hunting, riding and sporting tribe we now call the Mycenaeans who at some time in their warlike career had come into contact with the Minoan civilisation of Crete, and from the scant evidence we have from engraved gems or gold work and some rather suspect fragments of frescoes, they seem to have adopted the highly sophisticated fashion of tight waists and flounced skirts of the exotic Cretans. By the time of the Trojan War, now dated *circa* 1250 BC, the Mycenaeans may have changed their costume to that of other eastern Mediterranean nations with whom they traded but they disappeared into some Valhalla leaving little trace other than their blood-stained myths and the treasures of their early glory in their well sealed graves. So it is to a later generation of Greeks that we have to award the palm of original costume design. The conquerors and successors of the Mycenaeans were a very different people; still nomadic and pastoral the Dorians came around 1200 BC with their flocks from whose wool they probably made their clothes. It took Greece several centuries to emerge from the cultural eclipse caused by the invasion of the rustic Dorians and we have no means of knowing what they or the indigenous people looked like in the interval as all art seemed to die out. When, in the eighth century BC, the curtain of the Dark Ages is raised a little we have evidence, from a few archaic statues and vases from the islands, which shows that a 'Mediterranean style' had evolved from the two cultures. Women seem to have worn wrapped-round skirts and even woolly jumpers, or separate little capes or bodices, while the men had discarded all leg covering as unnecessary in a warm climate. Their garments appear shaped and sewn together, especially the short tunics worn by the young men – of the 1910 bathing suit variety – unlike the later styles which were draped. The fine climate and a new emphasis on Health and Beauty are certainly responsible for the next change, in the seventh century: a blossoming of a truly local style which consisted in the main of one garment and a wrap. The Greeks appear to have been so satisfied with this arrangement that, with the exception of exaggeration by width and pleating, the style remained static over many centuries.

The simplest garment, the *chiton* (of cotton and truly indigenous as the Ionic root-word implies) was a long shift for women and older men, and a short one for the young men who deigned to wear anything other than a cloak. The *chiton* was made from a rectangular piece of material folded in two and passed round the body, under the arms, with the opening at the right side. It was then pulled up, back and front, at equal distances from the sides and fastened on to each shoulder, leaving the arms free, and girdled round the waist. An alternative style for women was the Doric *peplos* which was worn in exactly the same way but had a wide flap turned over at the top, falling over the bosom and hanging down in two points at either side over the girdle. The earliest garments were severe, narrow and sometimes patterned all over. They can be seen on very early funerary vases worn by dancers or wailing women at a 'wake', with fullness bulging over a waistband either side and in some cases a bare leg protruding through the opening at the side.

Wraps were worn by both men and women; the most enveloping, the *himation*, was in early days a semi-circular piece of material draped with the points hanging down over each shoulder. Later it became a square wrapped round the body, thrown nonchalantly over the shoulder or demurely over the head, and was sometimes the sole covering for a man.

The *chlamydon* was a narrow shawl worn by women, pleated on to a band over the right shoulder and under the left arm, forming interesting folds to hang down over the *chiton*.

The *chlamys* was the short cloak fastened at the neck and was a favourite with young men. The airy-fairy Classical period of the fifth century BC exaggerated all these styles and widened the *chiton* so that it could be caught many times down the shoulders and arms to form sleeves when girded round the waist, and even round the armholes – as worn by that famous but rather dumb athlete, the charioteer of Delphi. This more florid style was known as the Ionic *chiton*, a creation of the gay and artistic Ionians who dominated central Greece, and was sometimes worn with a patterned *chiton*, as an underdress by actors.

The *peplos* was elaborated in width with a longer turn-over, so deep that it could be belted in like a jumper. The skirt of either garment was pulled up and bloused over one or two girdles, high under the bosom and again round the hips. It is obvious that the drapery and pleating of the clothes of the Classic period could only be arranged with fine muslin material, very possibly similar to the crepe cotton that is still made in Greece. The material was certainly coloured and the people more covered than their statues and vase paintings of gods, athletes and bright young things would have us believe. The figures from Tanagra of 300 BC are as amply dressed as any Victorian.

Hair styles in the early days were severe with flat curls on the forehead under circlets, for both sexes, with the rest pulled back and bunched at the nape of the neck. Neat pointed beards and moustaches were fashionable for all men in the early days and lasted for older men through Classical times. Women lifted their back hair after the sixth century BC in caps, bandeaux or diadems, back and front, that held the curls up and away from the neck.

The sane and graceful people of Greece had all the well made accessories of elegantly dressed people – the fine sandals, sun hats and parasols – which with the Classical dress were so much admired by less polished peoples that (in the first occasion of fashion-setting) we can see them repeated in the costume of Europe for many centuries to come.

570 B.C.          570 B.C.          445-450 B.C.          460 B.C.

## Greek Archaic and Classical Dress

*Drawn by Faith Jaques © a Hugh Evelyn Print*

PLATE II

# *The Etruscans* BC

With the Greeks playing the lead in the European drama of the last centuries BC, the character players may be said to have been the controversial Etruscans. Unfortunately they lost their script and can only speak through their rather sepulchral remains. We do not propose to enter into the intriguing game of Etruscology, which apparently has a way of sending its learned participants back to the bottom of the ladder at each gambit, but offer a few tentative observations on the known facts of these colourful people and attempt to show how their appearance was in a direct line in the evolution of costume and how they influenced their mighty successor, Rome. Who they were and where they came from is a matter that may be resolved one day: suffice to say that the north and west of Italy, especially around Rome, was occupied by a race of brown, energetic, well organised people living in the full-blown, luxury class from the seventh century BC without (and this is what foxes the pundits) any signs of having evolved from a more primitive, indigenous way of life. Etruria was a fine, wooded country excellent for farming and minerally rich. The fact that the Etruscans possessed a fierce, competent navy to ward off poachers on their sources of mineral supplies, allied to the abundance of gold and metal-work found in their tombs, leads us with no great detective ability to conclude that their wealth and prosperity arose from the bronze and iron trade. Situated as they were on the seaboard and at the crossroads of Europe, they diversified their interests by acting as middlemen for the luxury goods produced by the Greek colonies (well out of competition's way to the south of Italy), to the still barbarian people of the north. It was the same barbarians who, swooping down upon them in the fourth century, are blamed for having destroyed their monuments; but the Romans, having already copied pretty well everything of the Etruscan way of life, were not sorry to see their rivals make their final exit and quickly rubbed out all the surface traces of their civilisation that the barbarians had left. Happily for us the Etruscans had done themselves most extravagantly in their tombs and had a gay and natural line in fresco-painting, from which we may presume to guess how they behaved and what they looked like.

Life appears to have been so entrancing, and the sting of death so fearful, that every means were taken to ensure that the spirit carried down to the underworld all the dearly-loved symbols of the gracious life of 500 BC. Sour grapes prompted the severe attacks of moral indignation suffered by both Greeks and Romans on the matter of Etruscan *joie-de-vivre*, virtue not being a strong point in the social behaviour of either nation at that or any other time. From the paintings and reliefs on sarcophagi we gather that the idea of a 'good time' has not changed in 2500 years or so, and corresponds disturbingly with the humour of the mid-twentieth century, in the strong contrast of sensual fun-and-games with violence and morbidity.

Although we are no longer allowed to believe the story of the Greek historian, Herodotus, that the Etruscans came ready-made, as refugees from Anatolian Lydia, there are so many details of their costume and habits fitting in with this theory that we can only conclude that a large number of immigrants *did* come from the more advanced countries of the eastern Mediterranean. Searching after minerals, they brought their already developed culture with them and gradually integrated with the native, primitive metal-working population of Italy, eventually dominating it. After all, sky-scrapers and golf-courses appeared in Africa and America on what had been virgin soil fifty years earlier.

The lively tomb-paintings illustrate many aspects of Etruscan daily life and show us what the people liked doing best, dining, wining (with piped music) and sporting. With the exception of the athletes and young entertainers, everybody is very well dressed in long robes, hats and cloaks that bear no resemblance to the contemporary wear of their early neighbours in northern Italy but have a strong affinity with the Greek, Cypriot and Phoenician 'Mediterranean style' of the seventh and sixth centuries BC. It is the Etruscan footwear that is the give-away, with the very oriental turned-up toes that resemble so vividly those of another 'lost' race, the Hittites of Asia Minor.

These fancy boots became a popular export line, a craft that seems strangely to have become traditional in that part of northern Italy. Their hats, too, are most original and engaging – pointed or Phrygian caps, and little round sun hats, they were certainly eastern importations. Seeing what successful traders these people were, it is understandable that the Greek god Hermes, the protector of commerce, should have borrowed the Etruscan hat and winged boots. Comfortably settled in the centre of the trade routes of Europe, the Etruscans were in an ideal position to exchange ideas and luxuries from far and wide. Although there was constant bickering with Greece over the sovereignty of the seas, there is no doubt as to where the Etruscan aspirations lay, as their tombs testify – stuffed with Attic vases and treasures from the more refined culture. For grand as it may be, there is something coarse and provincial about a great deal of Etruscan art, with rather too much gold and rarely the delicacy of touch of the Greek workmanship. As time went by, the ways of life of the two cultures became even closer, with the adoption by the Etruscans of some of the Greek gods and a number of their pastimes, especially athletics. The passion for attending festivals is not new and parties of Etruscan youth could well have witnessed the Olympics and, as trade was carried on regardless of hostilities, it is possible that the latest pop-wear found its way to Etruria, accounting for the young men looking so very like the go-ahead Greeks. There were also the Greek colonies in southern Italy to be imitated, but in spite of these close ties the Etruscans kept their separate identity, which is especially evident in the costume of the older citizens, never becoming as open or flowing as the Greek fashions. Women and older men, up to the fourth century, wore long straight gowns which appear to have been sewn together on the shoulders and up the sides, sometimes three-quarter length over a pleated underskirt on top of which they draped the important cloak of a darker colour. The women, again in a later local tradition, often wore these over their heads while the men wrapped theirs tightly round the body and threw one end over the left shoulder. Colours were sombre and the garments do not appear to have been as heavily patterned as the Greek models. Wine and rust-reds, ochre and dull green with contrasts of cerulean blue made a beautiful range of hues but, of course, we can never be sure that the material dyes were the same as the pigments used for the frescoes, and clothes may have been quite differently coloured. The young men wore the tight tunics, bordered round the neck and hem as well as down the shoulder and side seams, that were so popular in Greece, and when the cult for body-freedom spread they went naked except for the shawls or short cloaks that appear to have been semicircular like the early Aegean cloaks. These were decoratively draped, usually with a swag down the back and the points hanging evenly over the shoulders, or they were thrown over the shoulder in pleats to swirl out when dancing. Pointed beards and long back-hair was the favourite hair-style for men, while both sexes often wore streaky curls hanging in front of the ear, with the rest pulled back and clubbed. Young men had short, rough curls worn rather more naturally than their Greek counterparts. Their jewellery was magnificent, with sets of diadems, earrings and necklaces in fine gold filigree that would be very popular wear today. The Etruscans eventually imitated every detail of Greek art and costume, but without the Greek obsession with an ideal image the effect is somehow quite different. Their down-to-earth nature is reflected in the attitude of a figure or the drape of a cloak, in the same way that their wonderful portrait heads of the third and second century BC are truly, speaking likenesses. It was this essence that was handed on to the Romans. In fact, the entire Roman ethos grew from the Etruscan way of life, omitting, only, a sense of humour. Rome itself was built by the Etruscans, who enclosed its seven hills within a defensive wall. The myth of its guardian spirit, the Capitolini wolf, and the emblems of authority, the fasces, were Etruscan conceptions. Censorious though the Romans were of Etruscan amusements, the gladiatorial games as well as their military organisation were borrowed from their predecessors and, last but not least, the most characteristic symbol of a Roman, his toga, was the direct descendant of the Etruscan *tebenna*.

6th century B.C.

530 B.C.

c. 500 B.C.

6th century B.C.

# Etruscan Dress

Drawn by Faith Jaques © a Hugh Evelyn Print

PLATE III

# Romans and Barbarians

## 1st – 4th century AD

Practically the whole of Europe benefited from Roman uplift which survived the onslaught of barbarians even after her monuments had collapsed and her power had been broken and forgotten. One of the most enduring of her legacies was her style of costume which, with Roman ubiquity, had been widely spread and had been accepted by all her subjects, anxious to show themselves no longer backward. The Romans had the advantage initially of being surrounded by people of great activity and ideas, the Etruscans and Greeks, and had been forcibly organised by the former into a small nation. There may be some reflection of truth in the legend that the Latini had originated from Troy, accounting for the spark of originality that marked them from their Italic neighbours, making them such apt pupils and transforming them from simple pastoralists living in villages on the 'Seven Hills' into a determined, world power. In their apprenticeship they suffered under three Etruscan kings (the last Tarquin rather overstepping the bounds of privilege in the matter of his subject, the virtuous Roman matron, Lucretia) and, having thrown them out, the Romans proceeded to form a very creditable type of benevolent oligarchy. The genius that prompted the spirit of nationhood involved them in a ceaseless fight for independent existence in Italy, which they subjugated after systematically liquidating every troublesome neighbour, even including the Greek settlements. It was contact with the latter civilised society that added a polish to a still rather rough and rustic community. It gave the Romans a taste for art (which culminated in their appropriating every piece of Greek sculpture they could lay their greedy hands on) and learning, which introduced them to the alphabet and the pleasures of philosophical debate. They already wore the robe and cloak of Etruscan costume and the short tunic for soldiers and young men, but the influence of Greece showed them how to wear these with grace and dignity. It has been thought that the main garment, the *tunica*, long or short, was always sewn up the sides, but many statues show tunics draped and fastened like the Greek *chiton*. Roman practical sense may have found that a made-up garment was more comfortable than the ideal they tried hard, at first, to imitate. The toga must have given them enough trouble without having to clutch at undergarments at the same time. This large and important cloak, a direct descendant of the semi-circular archaic Greek wrap adopted by the Etruscans, was finally enlarged and elevated to pomp and circumstance by the Romans. The toga was a badge of class and civic status belonging only to citizens. No slave was permitted to wear it; a freed man showed his condition by assuming it, and its denial was part of the punishment of a banished citizen. The Emperor wore a toga of purple wool, the Senators natural wool colour with a purple hem; the *equites* or knights (an exclusive set, this) had red or purple stripes, while the ordinary citizen wore plain white or the warm colours of natural wool. One end of the toga was probably secured in the waistband, at the back, to hold it while the material was brought round the body, under the right arm and thrown over the left shoulder in a wide band of several folds (very useful as a pocket or vanity bag, or as a cache by small boys). It was then brought round to the front again, sometimes over the head (by mourners or when sacrificing), and under the right arm with the end draped again over the left arm or shoulder. The dramatic effect with which the loose end could be waggled or swirled illustrates why no senator would dream of appearing before a tribunal without it. The regulations regarding the details of its drapery or colour could only have been conceived by a bureaucracy-loving people, and the headaches it must have caused to those citizens less fond of regimentation probably accounted for its replacement at the end of the fourth century by the *pallium*, of which more anon.

The robe under the all-enveloping cloak and the main garment of the working classes was the *tunica*, made of wool until the second century, when cotton and linen were brought from Africa and the east. It was worn long by women, to the ankles by men, or short if young or soldiering. The early garments were draped and caught on the shoulders exactly like the Greek *chiton*. The manner of girdling and the length suffered under yet another set of regulations, the discussion of which in the absence of any new variety became a hot debating point. This one considered a loose garment slovenly, the other declared girdling impracticable, and the long *tunica* was finally branded by Cicero as effeminate while the soldiers on duty in the cold north found the short skirts draughty and settled the matter by adopting the sensible trousers of their foes. Both sexes wore one tunic over another according to the weather. Unfortunately the Romans became slightly drunk with success under the Emperors, especially when they forsook their forthright, rational approach to external problems and fancied themselves as the romantic heroes of Greek epics. With an economy founded on slave labour from foreign conquests, Rome could afford every civilised luxury the world had to offer. Everything then became outsize and overstretched; bigger and grander architecture, baths and costume. Where hair styles had been simple, like those of Classic Greece caught back in a knot for women and short and smart for men, they rose in the second century to great heights as halos of curls, in serried rows, with numerous braids curled round the head at the back. Men's hair became fuller and wigs were worn, often of metallic thread, by both sexes. The *tunica* appears to have become more like a real robe, a long piece of material folded in two with a hole cut in the fold for the neck, and sewn down each side under the arms. It was girdled high by women and decorated most curiously with two vertical stripes, the *clavi* (once a single stripe down the front of senators' tunics), which again denoted the rank of the wearer, according to their width. This decoration later lost its classy significance and became worn solely by servants. Christians, as 'servants of God', rather deliberately wore these loose, horse-blanket-like robes and we may picture them in the Catacombs or going to martyrdom so inelegantly clad.

Pieces were added at the armholes in the third century, under the influence of the East, to form sleeves which gradually grew narrower towards the wrists. The sleeved shift, the *stola*, was generally worn by women under a sleeveless tunic, the *colobium*, which could be shorter than the under-

garment. Beautiful sandals showed off their feet but, again, held many pitfalls for the wearer in the regulations of prestige. We are not told if officials were appointed to control the length of robe or height of boot and see that no mean fellow overstepped his rank. The Emperors and Generals wore the nattiest footwear in fur-trimmed buskins decorated with animal heads on the turn-over tops.

The coming of the barbarians as conquerors showed the Romans a different type of costume. Every nation coming from the north or east wore leg coverings and their obvious advantages soon appealed to the practical Roman. The designation of *bracarius*, 'maker of breeches', was given to a tradesman in the time of Diocletian in the third century. Constantine moved the capital of the Empire of Byzantium (later Constantinople) in AD 330, to guard the eastern frontiers and to escape harassment from northern barbarians at home. Eastern materials and styles then made their way more abundantly to the west and soon the heavy togas gave way to the *pallium*, a version of the Greek *chlamys*, fastened on the right shoulder with a fibula pin and covering the left arm. The severe decoration of lines, the *clavi*, became decorative bands of embroidery in eastern designs of scrolls and circles, while the barbarians added their contribution to the new fashions in Celtic and Germanic repeat-patterns of spirals and interlocking plaits. Basic European fashion then appeared and, by the fourth century, Romans, barbarians and people of the East were all wearing a fairly uniform dress. Curiously enough, Britain may have been in the van of fashion at this time, as the powerful Constantine, son of an English princess, had lived there and the Vandal-cum-Roman general, Stilicho (seen in Plate III wearing the amalgamation of styles: Roman, barbarian and Byzantine in *tunica*, leg-coverings and patterned *chlamys*) had once been a commander of Roman legions in Britain.

*Erratum*
*Plate III: for* 260 AD *read* 1st century AD

A.D. 260

A.D. 395

## Roman Classical and Byzantine Dress

Drawn by Faith Jaques © a Hugh Evelyn Print

PLATE IV

# The Byzantines

## 6th century AD

If Napoleon and Hitler had regarded history a little more closely they might have realised how early in the European record the futility of world power had been proved. The Roman Empire by the fourth century was so fully stretched that many outposts had been abandoned and the situation at home was far from comfortable, with the constant hammering at the gates by Vandals, Goths and Lombards. Unable to contain the onslaught, Rome played at power politics and adopted the most persistent tribes as allies, admitting them into the army and within the frontiers as settlers, with the result that half the population of Italy became Germanic, even to the Emperors, by the end of the third century. Roman power was founded purely on military expansion and when the conquests ceased so did the flow of goods and slaves, and without cheap labour the national economy came to a standstill as no Roman did his own dirty work or had ever bothered about industrial exports to balance the country's expenditure. It can be said that the army never let the side down; the inclusion of barbarians even stiffened the morale and paid off in the end by defeating the worst enemy of European civilisation, the Huns. But the army was no longer supported by a capable republic. Emperors after contact with the East had acquired a taste for oriental despotism and divinity, and the people, deprived of their responsibility for social order, degenerated rapidly and allowed the most regrettable side of human nature to prevail.

In the general state of moral decadence and spiritual gloom the message of Christianity was heard, and answered the needs of man for a purpose and a hope for the future. It also, most conveniently at the time, advised the subject to submit to a ruler and allowed the ruler a divine right as God's Viceroy on earth – or so the scriptures were interpreted. To an astute character such as the Emperor Constantine the advantages of Christianity as a state religion were golden, so after many vicissitudes the Christians in AD 313 were granted freedom of worship. With the worthy object of starting a reformed Empire from a new centre (and Rome having become too un-comfortable with clamorous barbarians and old republicans antipathetic to despotic rulers) Constantine removed himself and his court to the East and rebuilt Byzantium, the 'New Rome', later to be called Constantinople. There, it was fondly hoped, all the elements of a great culture, Greek learning, Roman organisation and the new religion from the East could flourish. The result was a distinct bias towards the oriental type of life so favoured by the Imperial patrons. Architecture and art now copied the Persian style and, to fit in with the general conception, costume lost its Greek Classic simplicity and assumed an Asiatic ornamentation and splendour. The standard of magnificence reached its peak, two hundred years after Constantine, in the reign of the Emperor Justinian who, with the aid of his equally enthusiastic and decorative wife, Theodora, made the greatest contribution to Byzantine culture. By this time, costume had become formalised into a distinctive style. The long or short tunic, the *dalmatic*, now cut in the T-shape to form sleeves and sewn up the sides, was the principal garment of both sexes and was still covered by a semicircular or rectangular cloak. It was in the way the latter was worn, and the new venture into decoration, that Byzantine costume took on such a characteristic appearance. With all the lovely materials and the skill of embroiderers in the East to inspire, the 'New Romans' soon began decorating their still simply cut garments with bands of jewelled embroidery, and became so lavish that drapery was hardly possible and the line became stiff and solid. Exuberant to display the emblems of the state religion, women had pictures of the scriptures embroidered on their robes, much to the scorn of the Church Fathers. Damask patterned material was often used for both cloaks and tunics, the pattern taking the form of dots in squares or circles, or rosettes in scrolls of Persian inspiration. A favourite device was to fill the squares with the letters of the Greek alphabet, which to the unlettered held a mystical significance. True to the Roman spirit, however far from home, the new trend had to be systematised. Cloaks were caught up on a specified shoulder with the right type of pin for one's station. The front of the *pallium* had to be decorated, for nobles, with a peculiar square ornament, the *tablion*, which differed in colour and pattern according to rank. The only woman to wear this badge was the Empress, after the eighth century. That of the Emperor, of course, was heavily embroidered gold, on a purple *pallium*.

The *pallium* grew less important for civil dress and dwindled into a stole hanging like a wide embroidered band down the front of the tunic. It was carried over the right shoulder, under the arm and across the breast over left shoulder to the back, where it was slotted through its own loop and either allowed to hang in a tail or brought round to the front again over the left forearm. This complicated scarf treatment appears to have been the regular Consular style. The *pallium* then appeared as a wide tabard falling well over the shoulders like sleeves, with a space cut for the neck. The back flap could be pulled round in front of the figure, thrown over the left shoulder and belted in to look like a tunic, as we see on the stylish St Agnes in Plate IV, just showing a strip of white lining across the bosom. The vertical stripes, the *clavi*, were still used for decoration especially for official and religious garments, becoming in court dress heavily encrusted with jewelled embroidery in stylised floral and scroll designs. All these styles became formalised into ecclesiastical vestments – the dalmatic, stole and chasuble – to perpetuate an image of the founders of the Church. Oriental influence was perhaps greatest in the head-dresses. The Emperors and their consorts of the fifth century wore round crowns quite different in shape from the diadems of Classical Rome and the women adopted the turbans and veils of Persia, with jewelled side pieces dangling down in front of the shoulders like huge earrings. The wide jewelled collars are reminiscent of Egypt and very possibly were a fashion passed on from Alexandria, the centre of Greek culture until wrecked by Christian zeal at the end of the fourth century. Sandals gave place to beautiful shoes, pointed-toed in the Asian style, sometimes strapped or ankle-high, covered with pearl embroidery and fastened with jewelled buckles.

Huge sums were spent on goods from India and China, for the people of Byzantium had acquired a taste for the luxury of silk, and the glorious metal-woven materials added to the pomp of Imperial costume. In a crafty move to reduce overseas expenditure Constantine had managed to bribe two Persian monks to smuggle the eggs of silk worms out of China (in their beards it is said) and, with the technical aid of the holy brothers and a judicious previous planting of mulberry trees, was able to rear enough worms to start the silk industry in Constantinople from where it eventually travelled to Italy.

Byzantium's warlike neighbours the Phrygians (such as we see from a mosaic in Plate IV), the Parthians, Persians and Scythians, had come, way back in pre-history, from much the same stock as the Goths and Vandals who had been such a trial to Rome, and all appear to have worn leg-covering, or trousers, from a very early period. In the shape and comfort of these garments they were far in advance of the Romans, as can be seen from some finely woven pants found on a body preserved by the peat bogs of Jutland and dated to 80 BC. The Romans and Byzantines all adopted the style, although for a time the barbarian chiefs rather fancied themselves in the loose togas of Roman Emperors. The fashion was finally accepted and became an important part of basic European costume.

The very elements of Byzantine art – of which costume was a part – borrowed as they were from the stylised ornamentation of Persia and restricted by the formalised symbolism of early Christianity, made it static, but in the absence of any inspiration in the West, Byzantine culture acted as a bridge over the dark period between the glory that was Rome and the new awakening in the Middle Ages.

6th century        6th century        6th century        c. 550

# Byzantine Dress

*Drawn by Faith Jaques © a Hugh Evelyn Print*

PLATE V

# The Carolingians

When Rome resigned its role of schoolmaster and drill-sergeant to the rest of Europe, and Western civilisation slipped back into the unenlightened ways of the barbarians, learning just managed to exist on the slender life-line offered from a most unexpected quarter – the monks of Britain and Ireland. Christianity had been partly responsible for the downfall of Rome but in order to survive it had been found necessary to form an Establishment, and quite naturally the Founding Fathers of the Church adopted the only institutions they knew, those of the State and the religion it had helped to destroy. The gradual rise to temporal power by the Church was not altogether premeditated roguery on the part of the leaders of the Faith. The pagan conception of the priesthood, as a guide to ritual and as mediator between God and man, gave the Church control over all earthly behaviour and a great deal of earthly wealth, as the obedient converts, following divine advice to renounce all temporal possessions, handed over their property to the Church for better distribution. The system of Christian priesthood rested on the faith in the continuity of the Blessing and Charge, direct from Christ, to his disciples, and through them to the elders (soon to be called Bishops) of the Christian communities, which endowed them with a divine quality for spreading the word and guiding ignorant laymen. With the fear of imminent doom and the awful reckoning before St Peter at the Gates, penitents fled to solitude in caves and up pillars in the misguided but earnest endeavour to escape temptation by their fellow men. The contemplative life had always appealed to the East and with so many of the elements of Christianity that came from Byzantium the monastic life was introduced, with the two-fold purpose of bringing some constructive system into this early Hippydom, and of forming establishments where those so anxious for the holy life could fit themselves for the ministry by learning, while still renouncing worldly contacts. When the continent and Britain were overrun by barbarians and the strength of Christianity in Rome and Gaul was at its lowest ebb, scholars fled for refuge to the monastic schools of Ireland, as yet untouched by the pagan invaders. In the peace of sympathetic communities a means of teaching was developed, and flourished, by writing and illustrating the holy books. The art used was a curious, and now characteristic, mixture of the old Celtic geometric decoration, the queer animal and bird motifs picked up from the Scythians in eastern Europe, and the interwoven plaits of Roman and Byzantine design. The result was highly individual – especially when the Irish started plaiting the animals. With typical enthusiasm and success where other races need reforming, the Irish threw themselves into the battle against paganism with such zeal that by the beginning of the seventh century parts of France, Burgundy, Switzerland and Germany came under one of the most civilising forces in history, and Celtic Christian art became as strong an influence as that of Byzantium.

Meanwhile the Bishop of Rome, on the strength of spiritual descent from the Founder, St Peter, had become supreme head of the Church, giving back to the capital an even more fearsome position of authority than it had had under the Empire. Unfortunately the power and infallibility proved too much for mortal man to bear and with the difficulty of interpreting the Gospel, opportunities arose for the perpetration of a good many honest but tortuous theories (called heresies by the Establishment) and a great deal of blatant dishonesty. No twist of dogma was left undone that could further the power and advantage of the Church – as the unfortunate Christian Visigoths (but of the heretical creed of Arius) found to their cost when fighting the still pagan Franks. With the future control of the strong Germanic states in mind, the Frankish king, Clovis, was successfully persuaded to accept the faith (of the Roman creed of Athanasius) on the battlefield in return for the support of the Church, which apart from paying off in immediate victory put the Franks in the lead in all temporal matters in the north of Europe. The irony of the situation was that having accomplished the conquest of the Roman Empire, the barbarians, with little civilisation of their own, became absorbed in that of the people they had conquered and, through their conversion, came completely under the thumb of Rome in another guise, the Church. Theodosius, Emperor of both the Eastern and Western Empire, was made to do penance by the good Bishop Ambrose of Milan for his slaughter in the arena of seven thousand revolting Macedonians. That a proud ruler of Spanish Visigoth ancestry should submit to this humiliation is a proof of the fear of divine retribution only to be avoided by the dispensation of the Church – although he probably thought the game worth the candle.

With the downfall of Rome and no demand for work on the grand scale, as well as the restrictions put upon them by the Church, the arts declined in the West and continued only in portraying the Christian symbols (mostly for sepulchral purposes) in a touchingly naive but clumsily debased Classical form. No originality can emerge from a system, except from an opposition, but it needs a determined and influential figure to put the new ideas over. The Ostrogoth, Theodoric, King of Italy, in the early sixth century showed the first glimmering of individualism in the buildings of his capital at Ravenna, but he probably employed a Byzantine architect. Culture had to wait for another two hundred years for Charles, King of the Franks, to emerge and fancy himself the reincarnation of a Roman Emperor and ruler of Europe – indeed, as protector of the Roman Church (which though spiritually strong was physically vulnerable), a Holy Roman Emperor and a partner in the government of the world. This position of some importance and delicacy has rarely been successfully filled, but in Charlemagne the title 'Great' was not misplaced. To educate his people Charlemagne had to fall back on the ancient culture. Latin had been kept alive as a common language by the Church and the monastic schools and, as an example, the Frankish-speaking king struggled with declensions in his spare time; also, as a good Teuton with a higher regard for the importance of women than that of the Latin races, he ordered the academic education of his own daughters. It is due to this man of parts that a fresh interest was taken in building and, on the triple basis of Byzantine inspiration, Classical foundations and the native talent of the Goths for design and pattern, the first real Western type of architecture was created, which we now call the Romanesque style.

It will be noticed that nothing very exciting happened, in the fashion sense, in all these years owing to the strong restraint of the Church. It was probably due to Charlemagne that the Germanic dress was not swamped by the Eastern styles, as it is said that the rugged ruler only donned State clothes on two occasions in his life, for his coronation by the Pope in Rome and to meet the latter's successor, and he could be rather unkind to his followers who aped the Eastern court. His own successors, the Ottos, wore full Byzantine regalia for their official portraits but their people are depicted wearing the basic fashion of the time – short tunic, hose and cloak which altered little over several centuries. The loose hose, of very gay colours, were tied in with contrasting bands, in the old barbarian fashion, and the cloak was monotonously clasped on the right shoulder for years to come. Footwear did change with the introduction of half-hose or sock-boots, probably also of woollen cloth, which had fancy turned-over tops. Women began to have a more tailored look in shape-revealing gowns, often three-quarter length, with the exciting innovation of full bell sleeves over the tight ones of the under-dress. These, and the tunic, were edged with bands of embroidery in the Byzantine style. Also from the East came the new head-dress, influenced by the growing misgivings of the Church over the creation of Eve. A veil was now placed over the hair, which had previously been allowed to flow freely, and wrapped round the neck in the first *wimple*. For grand occasions this was topped by a turban made by twisting a long embroidered band round the head. With these novelties the fashion-conscious had to be content for another hundred years or more.

9th century                  c. 1000                  c. 1080-1150

# *Carolingian Dress*

*Drawn by Faith Jaques © a Hugh Evelyn Print*

PLATE VI

# The Normans and Romanesque Style

## 12th – 13th century

Although the Germanic barbarians had little to offer in the way of literate civilisation to their conquered people, they had one or two surprising natural qualities that added a different and improved spice to the character of the new nations. One was their attitude to women, whom they held in greater respect than did the Latin races or, alas, the Christian Church, which suffered them as an embarrassment. This characteristic inspired the bright, romantic movement by the Troubadours of southern France which, for the first time since the Christian era, took a very different view from the Church in the matter of human love. Another peculiarity of the barbarians was the fierce insistence on personal and political liberty which bore fruit in England in the Witan court, Magna Carta and Habeas Corpus. It was also responsible for the first democratic system of feudalism which only went sour, like chivalry, through human failure and excess.

England and France were certainly braced up by these invasions; the latter yet again in AD 911, by Norse pirates, when her rulers had become flabby and ineffectual. A century and a half later these same Norsemen, now respectable Norman Dukes, turned their attention to England and, taking it over completely, injected such a tonic of good government and business acumen into its muddled economy that before long its voice began to be heard in European affairs. William the Conqueror merely reinforced the laws of the country which were already feudal and, to the Normans, of a familiar kind, but he introduced something quite new to England, a system of big business. Painfully aware that war and the State must be backed by real money, William had to suffer his financial supporters (the Jew traders and money-lenders who had already linked the known world with a banking system) to accompany him and settle in his new kingdom, with the result that their capital boosted enterprise and made London a respected financial centre.

As well as for the zealous missionary monks, England was known abroad, from the seventh century, for several other useful commodities, the prin-cipal of which were tin and the fine wool from the sheep reared by the less venturesome agricultural brethren that was sold in all the markets of the Continent. Wool, until iron and coal were developed in the nineteenth century, cushioned the whole economy and was of such importance that the entire populace was somehow involved in its production. The real wealth, however, came from cloth-making, but although encouraged in England (the weavers were the first trade guild to receive a royal charter from Henry I, in the early thirteenth century) it could not compete with the rich cloth cities of northern France which, the English kings noted with envy, paid heavy taxes to the Crown for civic privileges. It must have been rather confusing at times for these monarchs to know which side they were on, as French dukes or English kings, and with wool clouding their usually astute judgment, King John lost Normandy and Edward II embarked on the war that was to last one hundred years – all to further the English wool trade in Flanders.

The Normans gave more to England than a chance to enter an early Common Market; they brought a refreshing urbanity to the home-spun little island, not, let it be said, through the uncouth early kings but through their family connections, the Norman princes who had spread with such rapidity through Europe and from the eleventh century were lording it over the centre of civilisation, southern Italy and especially Sicily. Lapping up the oriental luxury and art of the displaced Arabs, as well as the learning and sophistication of the Byzantine Empire they did their best to supersede, they had plenty of new ideas to hand on to their ruder brethren in the north. Through acquaintance with Moslem art and architecture, building took on a new look and became more adventurous, and through contact with Byzantine polish and glamour, costume design had the first real fillip it had received for centuries – and the English began their rather grudging dependence on France for fashion trends. The over-tall figures clad in stylised much-pleated robes on Romanesque and early Gothic cathedrals are merely a translation into stone of the elongated, impressive images of Italian Byzantine art, which the monkish illuminators of Anglo-Norman manuscripts also used to great effect, dressing their figures in the swirling, form-revealing lines of contemporary costume, often caricaturing it. The eastern influence did give back to men a dignity they had lost in the first flush of barbarian domination, in the longer outer robe which, with its more important sleeves and tight lacing up the back or at the sides, became a popular alternative to the rather skittish Germanic tunic. Knights even wore these long robes over their chain-mail and to avoid loss of dignity the skirts were slit up the front or at the sides. In the first instance of dagging, or mantling (cutting the material like a fringe), long cuts to the depth of twelve inches appear all round the skirt of a knight in a Swiss manuscript dated about 1175; so this queer fashion, which lasted over three hundred years and was at its most exaggerated height in the early fifteenth century, may have been inspired by the need for leg-room. Semicircular cloaks lost their regimented shoulder fastening and were caught together at the throat in front with a gem-set brooch or by cords looped round studs at either side. In the matter of hair the Normans rather surprisingly adopted the English fashion. As barbarians they had accepted the short crop of the Romanised Franks amongst whom they settled. In England they were faced with the embarrassing fact that only a serf's head was clipped, and realising that the complete reversal of an accepted theory is impossible they grew their own hair to the required prestige length, only to receive rude criticism on returning to their homeland. Henry I had to suffer an episcopal trim up the back and sides, so greatly did long hair and beards offend French religious, and civil, good form.

As the Byzantine styles became more popular, longer hair and well-trimmed beards, often forked, became accepted, until the fourteenth century when a more youthful appearance began to be the vogue.

To the beginning of the twelfth century can be traced the first individuality about the design of women's clothes. The smartest fashions from the Byzantine east tended to be sexless, the long-robed men receiving the same sort of heated criticism that the mid-twentieth century is used to hearing. As if to live up to the new concept of the 'ideal woman' (the sex-game conjured up by the Troubadours of southern France) feminine clothes suddenly developed an allure they had never previously shown in Europe. Bodices became tight across the chest and, so as to show the lines of the figure to advantage, waists were defined and the wide skirts (often with inset gores) dropped into heavy trains which pulled the material closely to the body in movement. The train was an innovation of the Middle Ages, Classical clothes having barely touched the ground evenly all round. Necklines were immodestly scooped out and not always covered by a wimple, and to balance the train long pieces which fell to the feet were added to the wrists of tight sleeves. The frequency with which the 'scarlet woman' appears in illuminations of this period, clad in all these exaggerated details, leads us to surmise that they were as much relished as censured by contemporary moralists. Both sexes look a bit tight over the chest, which may be due to the difficulty of making sleeves fit closely without cutting them separately. The waistline began to droop by 1150, heralding the long-bodied, hip-fitting line of the fourteenth century, and was accentuated by a heavy belt or girdle. The northern people contributed quite a few ideas to fashion on account of their climate. The barbarians had worn skins as protection: now in the twelfth century their descendants began to use fur for both warmth and decoration. Cloaks were lined with marten and squirrel and the beautiful ermine gave its life for the comfort and prestige of the aristocracy. So fine had the treatment of pelts become that several kinds of fur could be superimposed on the outside of cloaks in a pattern. Coats-of-arms, we are told, were originally these patterns of fur, and as shields were even decorated with it the terms used for hues and devices in heraldry still keep the names of different furs.

1175–1200                                1150                                1275–1300

# Romanesque and Norman Dress

*Drawn by Faith Jaques © a Hugh Evelyn Print*

PLATE VII

# Chivalry, Troubadours and Minnesingers

## Early 14th century

With the advent of chivalry in the twelfth century, it was as though Eve raised her eyes from her eternal spinning, gave a pat to her hair and reached for the most tempting apple. The Christian people had been so feverishly absorbed in the destination of their souls (in between the most blatant backsliding) and so sure that the day of judgment was to come at the first millenium that a certain pessimism can be detected in their behaviour, much reflected in art and literature, up till that time. Even the goings-on in Constantinople and the vicious fun at the French courts have an air of being moments of defiant enjoyment snatched out of a doomed eternity. As the anxious moment passed and the world appeared to go on turning much the same as usual, Christians began to look upon their religion with a little more faith and less fear and to argue that perhaps the human instincts were God-given. This was going a little further than the Church intended, but in the new Age of Optimism there were those confident enough to make a long nose at the Establishment, and woman came in for a share in this early 'back to nature' movement in a most curious way. Chivalry, the peculiar phenomenon combining physical toughness, unrequited love and a propensity for going on long, fruitless journeys (which has occurred so often in history that it would seem to answer a very deep-felt want in man), had its roots in a very practical and crafty measure for ensuring loyal support to a leader in times of war. The Germanic tribes were apt to be a bit independent and, as free men, fought for any leader who appeared to be the most successful in the offensive. This behaviour was too risky when the tribes had settled and become nations with their own land and property to protect. The system of warfare, started by the Franks, of heavily armed, mounted knights and their retinues, introduced the need for trained men and expensive equipment; and so as to be able to rely upon this support with certainty, some tactical wizard thought up a scheme that provided an occupation exactly suited to the mentality of hearty young men and, by making the grade so difficult of attainment, created an exclusive profession with fierce competition to join

its ranks. It was probably the genuine idealism and enthusiasm, present in so many young men, that raised the profession in the initial stages to something above mere physical prowess and stressed virtues and talents, but one has the sneaking feeling that the new concept of 'honour', that allowed no fickle changes of loyalty, and the mystic ritual of initiation were strategies to bind a man more securely to his obligations.

The versatile and chivalrous bards of the southern French courts, with their romance tales of love and valour, added yet another element to the complicated requirements of knighthood. Already dedicated to championing the weak, the knight now had sanction for sensual love to be exalted to a virtue, and the previously despised female suddenly found herself elevated to the position of being the inspiration of all sorts of idealistic achievements and the object of male homage, of a rather dubious sort. The French, of course, enthusiastically pursued every possibility of their intriguing new philosophy, only to discover that human nature did not take kindly to the rules of chivalry *and* the platonic ideal. The Germans prudently played safe and stuck to the original theory of homage to woman in general, while the English, one suspects, very quickly separated the sports from the pastimes. The success of the idea of fellowship and loyalty did not pass unnoticed by the Church which quickly took advantage of the enthusiasm for the movement by forming semi-religious military brotherhoods, the Hospitallers and the Templars who proved so useful in the early Crusades. A boy had to start early in his training for knighthood if he hoped to reach the desired standard – a mixture of the Archangel Michael, an Olympic champion and a pop singer – by the age of twenty-one. The Victorian image of the perfect knight would appear to have been based on the ideal, rather than the practice, of chivalry, judging by the records of some of its members. As the romantic homage to women was all part of an elaborate game it made no lasting difference to their status in a hard society; and as the original object of the exercise, the highly trained and heavily armoured cavalry, was defeated by the English bowmen at Crecy and the determined Swiss peasants at Sempach on their flat feet, the whole artificial structure collapsed.

It did have an enormous influence on the decorative appearance of the Middle Ages and so concerns us here. The need for symbols distinguishing different knights and their followers, before the days of organised regiments and uniform, inspired the conceit of claiming a flower, or animal, as a personal badge which was displayed first on a banner, then on shields and later, with slight arrogance, on clothes. The Frankish kings may have started the custom in Europe by what, for them, would seem to be a rather sissy habit of carrying a branch of white iris or lily as a sceptre at a coronation, which became their badge and, afterwards, the arms of France. When surnames became necessary to avoid muddle over generations and families, other than by adding 'son' after the first name, these whims of the nobles were used to distinguish them and their descendants, and illustrate how individuals were beginning to influence fashion. The English took to armorial bearings in a big way through the rather showy type, Geoffrey of Anjou, whose whimsy of wearing a sprig of broom, the *planta genesta*, in his helmet or cap gave the name Plantagenet to his descendants, a line of English kings, in the same way that the lions on his shield, the first recorded arms, became royal insignia.

Another factor that made clothes more interesting in the middle of the thirteenth century was the rise of the professional and merchant class. More wealth amongst these people meant larger cities and the opportunity to show off one's prosperity, and with ideas stimulated by travel, fashion was no longer restricted to the nobles. The French had most of the good ideas and were imitated by the less lively-minded nations who sometimes took a quarter of a century to catch up with the latest fashion. It is obvious that the movement of chivalry did make life more human, and amusing and freer for women, as we see from the jolly little illustrations to the love poems of the Minnesingers, the German version of the Troubadours. Women took part in sport, especially hawking, beginning their long history of horsemanship, and it is encouraging to know that the rules of chivalry gave them the opportunity occasionally to make the superior male look very silly.

Both sexes wore the long robe (the woman's only distinguished by a train) with wide or dangling sleeves over a tight-sleeved contrasting undergarment. At the end of the thirteenth century a new style appeared, the *surcoat*, of a pinafore shape, clearly inspired by the comfortable sleeveless tunic worn by the knight over armour. This was sometimes decorated with the family arms, in two halves, or with horizontal bands, like the charges on shields. The undergarment became more closely fitting as the armholes of the surcoat were enlarged until, by 1340, in France and England the sides were cut down to the hips, in the fashion that lasted for women's ceremonial wear all through the next century. There were innumerable buttons down tight sleeves, at openings and even up the sides of surcoats, which began to have hoods and little capes for men. Necklines were lower and the really chic wore them in a wide boat-shape. The more conservative women still wore wimples under the chin, filling in the neck opening, the English from their church monuments looking particularly 'county' and prudish. As the religious orders made a uniform for their nuns out of the most modest contemporary dress, French women noticed how frumpish the veil looked when draped flat over the head and, as early as 1250, started to wear little pork-pie caps, with great style, to give height, in very much the same way as stiffeners have been used in the twentieth century to lift the eternal peasant scarf away from the hair.

In these definitely shaped garments, button fastenings and collars on front-closing cloaks we see the last of Classical clothes, except perhaps for the all-purpose garment, the hooded robe that the religious orders had made from the *paenula* (Roman cloak) and the wide *dalmatica*. Clothes were now so close-fitting that they could no longer be put on over the head and early in the fourteenth century the hooded robe was open right down the front making, for all and sundry, the first real coat.

*Chivalry, c. 1325*

PLATE VIII

# The Crusades and Gothic Style

### Early 14th century

It will have been noticed that styles of costumes changed at snail's pace up until the thirteenth century, fifty years, or even one hundred, producing perhaps a revolutionary type of sleeve or cloak-fastening. Stagnation in ideas for dress reflects to perfection the social atmosphere of the period. It is only in an advanced society that people dress (or undress) to express personal ideas and attitudes, and inspiration is slow to materialise when encouragement is limited. It takes a great upheaval for people to change their ideas and the twelfth century afforded just that shake-up. One of the strongest passions in man appears to be his desire to be constantly on the move, at the closest quarters possible with his fellow men. No matter how hard the way, from the Children of Israel to the weekenders and protest marchers of the twentieth century, people have walked and ridden in great hordes on any pretext, but mainly for the questionable joy of being together. As ordinary travel was expensive and dangerous, pilgrimages were the thing in the Middle Ages, making a good excuse to leave a family or tiresome job as well as having the extra benefit, even if not taken as a penance, of sanction by the Church. Chaucer's crowd enjoyed the going as much as the arriving and, what is more, entertained themselves on the way. For a really big exodus the conditions at home must be unsatisfactory and the pretext fanatically idealistic. Both these situations prevailed in the twelfth and thirteenth centuries, resulting in the enormous tours of the Crusades. Kings might flout the Pope but the common man was so bowed down at this time under the weight of heavy penances by the Church that the prospect of indulgences, covering many years out of Purgatory as a reward for taking part in the campaign, very quickly rallied the crowds, in the same way that religious chivalry, the prospect of high adventure and the hope of spoils from the fabulous East, started the nobles packing.

Not only knights and armies made the journey: wives, sisters and friends took to the road and shared the men's experiences. A veil is best drawn over the outcome of these violent, hysteria emoted exercises from which few returned with anything other than empty pockets and tropical diseases, and whose only success was in cementing the national hatred between the Christian participants that appears to have lasted to the present day. One leader is said to have spent as much time separating the French and the Germans (originally one tribe of Franks) as he did in fighting the Saracens. All were not brutes or Philistines, however, and a few intuitive men must have kept their eyes open while in the eastern lands. There were all the treasures of Constantinople, the tributes of centuries, to admire, but the strange buildings, the pattern and decoration on tiles and pottery and the graceful flowing robes of the oriental countries were found more exciting and an inspiration to experiment with the new forms at home.

It is a miracle that any of the more sensitive souls ever did make the return journey, but back home they must have come for new styles began to appear in art and costume – and their effigies to grace the great cathedrals that rose up as a thank-offering for God's supposed backing of their venture and their safe return. As usual it was France who pioneered the way. Already more active in the Crusades and leading in European scholarship in Paris, contact with new elements positively drew sparks of brilliance from them. The introduction of windmills to Europe from Syria in the twelfth century was a useful but mundane matter compared with the result of using the pointed Arab arch in architecture. As art, until the fourteenth century, was exclusively in the service of the Church the novel ideas were tried out in the designs of the new cathedrals. The shape of the old Roman basilica had done duty for many centuries for Christian churches, the Romanesque style adding a transept to form a cruciform shape and crowning the intersection with a dome to give height. The weight of the ceiling rested on solid walls and piers, and even with rounded arches to break the straight lines the effect is four-square.

Though the behaviour of our medieval ancestors was in many ways deplorable, their achievements prove their intentions to have been lofty and fixed on a heavenly goal. Anxious to direct the worshipper's thoughts up-wards and finding the pointed arch gave the impression of greater height, the engineers of early thirteenth-century France swotted up their geometry, grappled with the new problem and produced miracles of vaulting, with arches of different spans, all rising to the same elegant point, to direct the eye upward. To prevent this delicate vaulting from collapsing (many did), buttresses were built into the walls to push against the thrust of the arches and carry the weight downwards, completely altering the appearance of the buildings. Where there had been wide wall surfaces for frescoes the narrow spaces between the buttresses called for windows, with the result that the whole interior became slender and lighter. The new look, which has been named Gothic, gradually pervaded all the visual arts. The craft of stained glass developed to fill the tracery of pointed church windows; painting, no longer needed to tell the Bible story by frescoes, became more widely practised, yet more intimate, as pictures on panels, and sculpture acquired grace while conforming to the upward-straining ideal. Last, but not least, fashion reflected the same spirit, demanding slender figures to wear close-fitting clothes and helping the aim with mounting head-dresses. Women had already raised the veil on top of the head and now, with real dash, they trained their plaits in vertical cables over each ear, surmounting the sculp-tured shape with stiff circlets and veils, often pinning up the wimple to the plaits on either side of the face. It was a simple step further to enclose the plaits with cauls of net and, as the trend was ever upward, to hold out the veil with wire supports later in the century. The pinafore-shaped surcoat remained popular for the whole of the fourteenth century, gradually becom-ing closer-fitting and, with a waistcoat-shaped fur front, very grand cere-monial wear when it had ceased to be the daily fashion. Worn by highly respectable matrons in the early fourteenth century it was still semi-fitting but cut with a wide swing to flute in heavy folds and fall back into a long train. The centre back-and-front seams cried out for parti-coloured treat-ment and decorating by halved and quartered arms. Lady Luttrell is seen charged with her husband's three birds and her own grand, family lion rampant; daughter-in-law Constance is, suitably, less nobly emblazoned.

The shape of armour appears to have dictated the line of men's clothes far more than the design or whim of an individual in the thirteenth and four-teenth centuries. Under a tunic and leg-covering of chain-mail a man wore a loose linen shirt and long hose tied up to short pants like baggy bathing drawers. Painful experience must have caused the long surcoat to be shortened to mid-thigh length with the increasing use of spurs and stirrups and as pieces of plate armour were introduced, at the beginning of the fourteenth century, to protect the legs above and below the knee. The heavy sword-belt drooping on to the hips gave the long-bodied line which became fashionable in about 1320 and lasted till the end of the century. This shortened tunic became progressively closer to the shape of the figure as it was made in leather to wear over chain-mail (we do not hear how many knights died of apoplexy), and, laced up the sides, it was called the *jupon*; later, buttoned down the front, it became the *cote-hardi*, both garments becoming fashionable civilian wear. Sir Geoffrey Luttrell was one of the lucky ones to return from the east and is seen here, some few years after the Crusades, clad in mail and the shortened surcoat. He is not about to depart for war but is again tempting Providence by engaging in the equally silly pastime of jousting.

Hats became very popular: pork-pie, tea-cosy and Robin Hood shapes, they were generally worn over a hood but these were lately taking on a new look, pulled right down and worn as a collar with the head pushed right through the face opening. The hood's peak was lengthened until it became a long tube to twist round the neck and drape over the shoulder and, matching the long dangling ends on sleeves, was known by the delightful name of *liripipe*.

*The Crusades, 1340*

Drawn by Faith Jaques © a Hugh Evelyn Print

PLATE IX

## *The Italian Early Renaissance*

### *Early 14th century*

The great upheavals that were caused by the Crusades had the effect of altering social conditions in quite unsuspected parts of Europe and of starting a far-reaching and brilliant cultural phase. Inspired genius may exist in a garret but is much more likely to flourish if given good square meals, patronage and stimulation, and the change that came about in the fourteenth century began to offer these pleasant conditions. Society, until then, was strictly divided by the feudal system, backed by the Church, into various classes, forming a collective organisation from which the individual could only with great difficulty cut himself loose. With the exception of wandering minstrels and a few pedlars, every man was bound to this self-supporting community surrounding the court and castle of his lord. There were no independent craftsmen or merchants, as the guilds formed a strong trade union to keep out any intruders into their particular districts. The Crusades started the rot in blind faith in religion (which had appeared rather to let the side down in dealings with the Arab and in just reward to the faithful) and the new democratic type of warfare began to sound the knell to feudalism and chivalry. But just as important was the impetus given by these quasi-religious-military pilgrimages to independent intellectual enquiry and the revival of Classical learning through contact with Arab translations of the Greek masters. More important still was the accumulation of wealth in the hands of the men who stayed at home. Italy, which took a relatively small part in the actual campaigns of the Crusades, emerged by far the most triumphant of the European participants for the simple reason that her maritime towns and their fleets were conveniently situated to convey the vast armies on the shortest route to the east and to supply, at exorbitant rates, the necessary stores and equipment. The demand created inspiration; talent, hitherto unsuspected, developed in the backward Italian people, in shipbuilding, armoury, textile making and food production. So, with money flowing abundantly, urban life expanded and, with wealth in a new class of independent citizens, merchants and professionals to support lay scholars, the seeds of the Renaissance were nourished and Italy began her artistic and commercial domination of Europe. The northern people have always taken their religion suspiciously, regarding it as a penance rather than a comfort and making changes violent and painful, the Germanic races being specially prone to fly off the handle in exploring and analysing every theory in depth, generally at great cost physically and spiritually. The Italians, on the other hand, accepted the promise and ritual of the Church with grace and enjoyment, even reconciling the new philosophy of their Humanists to the existing religion without too much struggle. The ideas of Dante and Petrarch, based on Classical rationalism (so frowned upon by the clergy) were revolutionary enough, with their new look at man's instincts and impulses (again considered by the Church as instruments of eternal damnation) and his spiritual and social place in nature and society, but the humanity and reasoning of their teaching and personalities softened the impact against tradition and influenced every phase of life, saving it from violent revolution and the vulgarity of material success. There was also the lucky coincidence that a strong artistic talent lay dormant in the northern Italians, inherited from their arty-crafty Bronze Age forebears, the Lombards, which suddenly awoke and broke away from the rigid rules of Byzantine art. Although at the onset only used for ecclesiastical decoration in Italy, it was the first effort for lay expression as opposed to that laid down by the clergy and could only have developed in a country where material wealth began demanding civic and domestic art. Giotto created a new form of illustration in his frescoes by disregarding the flat symbolism of the Byzantine style and giving human feeling and movement to his figures which, to his contemporaries, must have been as exciting as a film or strip cartoon. The new Humanism in art developed in other countries where economic independence through trade gave it encouragement, but the effect was rather different, as we shall see later, in the rise of Burgundy to power.

The same gracious spirit of the early Renaissance is very apparent in

Italian costume of this period which while following the general trend of ideas always had a soft and natural look. There was already a great richness of materials, the industry having become very advanced in the fourteenth century. The Norman lords of Sicily had early indulged themselves in gorgeous clothes and had set up Greek weavers in Palermo for this purpose, whence they spread north to develop the silk industry in Florence and Genoa. Even printed material was being used, partly influenced by the import of oriental stuffs and by the new use of wood-block patterns discovered by the mechanically-minded Germans in their search for a means of printing script.

The general line of clothes (influenced by armour which became close-fitting at the beginning of the fourteenth century) was long-bodied and followed the natural shape of the figure, becoming slightly exaggerated as the heavy sword and purse weighed down the girdle low on the hips. This accessory, with the dangling sleeves, gave the distinctive character to fashion from about 1340 to the end of the century. The girdle, which had a peculiar significance, probably due to its association with the sword and purse, was thought to bestow upon its wearer all sorts of virtues and advantages and was given great prominence in the costume. Heavy metal embroidery was used and, when the wearer could afford them, many precious stones. There was a good deal of hokum about this fashion as, we regret to record, it has been found that imitation gems were often used. Whether or not the same faith was put in their magical properties, they were good enough to bury with kings and sufficed the needs of the new bourgeois class who now affected the aristocratic fashions. Italian robes, for both sexes, were more ample than those of their contemporaries in the north. Women's gowns were made with fitting sleeves and the tops were certainly cut separately from the full skirts hanging in folds and attached without gathers to a low waistline. Tongue-shaped gores were also introduced to give width to the hems without bulk over the hips. Braid-trimmed boat-shaped necks, and sometimes seams, were used, and

the gowns often fastened right up the front like men's *cote-hardis*. The surcoat seems to have been worn less in Italy, probably because the climate made the extra warmth unnecessary. The long *cote-hardi* with hanging sleeves gave dignity to older men and was much favoured by scholars. Short cloaks and little shoulder capes with the new high-standing collars were worn over long gowns or the short *cote-hardi* by younger men.

Up to the twelfth century clothes in their entirety had been made at home by the women, who spun and wove the material and finally did the cutting and sewing. As the shape of garments became more intricate craftsmen were called in and the clothing industry came into being, developing so rapidly that in the thirteenth century tailoring guilds began to specialise in different garments and, by the fourteenth century, men's and women's clothing were made by separate professionals. It would be intriguing to know who had the first fashion sense, the vain and talented lady or a craftsman offering a new shape. More emphasis and variety was given to headgear. Hoods were now folded to look like caps and had their points elongated, a fashion that set the tradition for court jesters, who could have extra fun with the long *liripipes* on their horned hoods that were derived from the animal masks of mummers.

It was in the arrangement of hair that the Italian women differed most from the women of northern countries. They used the now universal style of plaits but allowed them to form a soft coronet on the top or back of the head in contrast to the French, English or German women who dragged the hair from the forehead and made the braids conform to an angular frame for the face. Veils and wimples, too, were worn less than in the north, the young women setting a style for every arty movement ever since (up to the mini-skirted girls of the 1960s), with their soft, loose-hanging locks falling to the shoulders from a centre parting. Men wore a short bob rolled into the nape of the neck and pointed beards made a reappearance, but the fine drooping moustaches of the British barons were not often seen on the more youthful-looking Italians.

*Italian Early Renaissance Dress, 1325-1335*

Drawn by Faith Jaques © a Hugh Evelyn Print

PLATE X

## English Peasants

### Early 14th century

The fourteenth century was not only remarkable for the great cultural advance in Europe but marks the occasion of England's emancipation from France and the start of her rather pugnacious career as a separate nation. It also happened to be a time when the first clear picture emerges of the individuals who made up the Island Race, apart from official records of the rather questionable doings of a line of kings, in the religious poem of *Piers the Ploughman* and from the autobiographies of Chaucer's Pilgrims. Something like that particular line of artistic and emotional expression in which the English have always excelled, the critical and topical cartoon that has made *Punch* such a splendid documentary, also began to sparkle on the vellum pages of manuscripts, surprisingly drawn by monks or priests to illustrate religious books. The Church in England had begun to reform itself from the licentious days of the wine-bibbing monk or friar who had been ordered to get out, work for and mix with the people. They were still practically the only educated members of the community; the grammar schools that existed were maintained by the monasteries or guilds for the sole purpose of turning out more clerks in holy orders to form an Establishment, as schoolmasters, civil servants and all those indispensible fillers of routine jobs that entail a knowledge of the three R's. Under the circumstances their unclerical behaviour and experience can be accounted for and the illuminating little pictures, even on monastic manuscripts, can be accepted as true observations of contemporary life. Some priests were more fittingly employed as chaplains or tutors to lordly families, and if blessed with a talented pen or brush and an observant eye, the result was an entertaining *Luttrell Psalter* or the *Rous Roll* of Warwick. The former not only describes the life of a knight and his family but illustrates in great detail the pursuits and pleasures of his henchmen and shows how advanced the English people had become materially, especially in their clothes, costume being the surest sign of prosperity and human self-assertion.

The situation in England looking so good, the Norman rulers settled for naturalisation and, becoming more insular than the ancient Anglo-Saxons, replaced French as the official language by the mixed English tongue and asserted their independence of their motherland by challenging France's commercial and martial might. With national independence confirmed, the Englishman then began his claim for the democracy that has made him so unique and peculiar to other nationals. The English peasant was just beginning to gain his freedom from serfdom by buying himself out of obligatory days of service to the landowner (who also found the system of payment by wages more satisfactory than forced and unwilling labour) and was able to concentrate on the cultivation of his own strip of arable land, ordained to him under Anglo-Saxon law. The careful husbandman was able to add the strip of his thriftless neighbour to his own and gradually create the new class of independent yeoman farmers, soon to rise, like the Paston family, to the highest positions in the land.

Another source of economic advance was in the good English sheep that multiplied so obligingly on the grasslands of the mild-climated isle. Wool, quite simply, became the 'staple' of the English economy and, as suggested elsewhere in this History, the donor of this prosperity might have made a more suitable national emblem than the lion. Had it been, perhaps the obstinate British assertion that the Empire was founded upon trade, rather than on aggression, might have carried more weight, as there is no argument that men risked unknown places and the most unlikely climates for the promotion of new markets for their valuable commodity. The production and marketing of raw wool and fine cloth absorbed the energies of the major part of the population, with the natural wealth well distributed between the estates of the lords temporal and spiritual and the common grazing ground of the modest peasant. With such close family ties with France and a steady demand for English wool the establishment of a central market for the sale of the wool had been easy. A steady export trade was of double advantage to the State, bringing in valuable foreign currency and a heavy export duty from the English merchants for the privilege of selling their goods abroad. It is unfortunate that greed crippled the golden goose in the futile attempt, in the Hundred Years War, to oust France from its control of the continental trade, and left England with only a tenuous foothold in Calais for its market of the 'staple'. Wool was the engrossing object of Englishmen's lives up till the industrial age, entering into their daily speech with expressions such as 'spin a yarn', 'fine-drawn', 'tease', etc., that we still use today. A new nation was founded in Australia on the cultivation of sheep and it is curious to note that when at its lowest ebb, after the Second World War, the only export line the British had to offer, that needed no sales promotion, was our good old standby – fine woollen suiting. In the fourteenth century the Englishman's whole appearance was affected by wool. He enjoyed meat and milk more often than other continentals from the numbers of sheep and other cattle on his extensive grazing grounds and he went better shod from their skins, while his clothes developed a national characteristic from the availability of good woven cloth.

The short tunic was the most practical wear for the working man and had continued in use without much change over centuries. Following the lead from France (with whom, in spite of wars and Crusades, there was constant contact) waists became lower and were accentuated by heavy belts carrying the purse or weapon. Working clothes were still worn wide enough to pull over the head and with slits up the sides for ease in walking, but by the four-teenth century had become so sophisticated as to be lined with a contrasting colour. A shorter, wide-shouldered sleeveless surcoat was sometimes worn over the tunic for extra warmth. As clothes became less of a bundle, the practical coat shape became common wear, hugging the figure by front-fastening and with close-fitting sleeves. These, since material would never have been woven so wide, were made by adding narrow pieces at, or below, the shoulders. Leg-coverings became of importance, both sartorially and practically, as tunics became shorter. They were made in strong cloth with seams up the back like leggings and, with or without feet, were hitched up to the breeches or tied to a string round the waist. Very often loose hose were made in soft leather for riding or rough wear. Footwear, too, had become more complicated and better fitting, either in cloth with leather soles, or entirely in leather, as trim ankle boots or fancy shoes with a hint of the coming Gothic fashion of long, pointed toes. Gloves had been the height of fashion from Byzantine times, but as all these luxuries were made by the country-folk and craftsmen they soon found their way into working costume and more practical use.

A liking for hats seems to have been common to all classes in this period that marks the beginning of true fashion design, with intentional fantasies and exaggerations to come. The high-crowned, wide-brimmed style, in felt, was the most popular, especially for travellers or pilgrims, with the brim pulled down over the eyes for protection from sun or rain, but was often worn in reverse, like a souwester. This style took the place of the large, shallow, round hat worn by travellers even from Classical times which, incidentally, was adopted by Cardinals in 1252 as a symbol of a pilgrim. The pork-pie shape, also in felt, became a classic style but with the slit brim it foreshadowed the hats of a much later date. Hoods and wimples were worn under hats, the women often wearing a pointed hood over a draped veil.

The line of a working woman's dress followed the fashionable shape – close-fitting top and long-sleeved *kirtle*, or robe, laced up the back. She, too, wore the surcoat, belted low with heavy purse or bunch of keys. In the *Luttrell Psalter* we see the first evidence of typical English country smocking, a method of gathering material by embroidery on the front of the very serviceable apron. The distaff (under the woman's arm even while she feeds the chickens) gave the name 'spinster' to unmarried women, as it was the daughters of the house or useful maiden aunts who usually prepared the thread for weaving.

*English Peasant Dress, 1340*

Drawn by Faith Jaques © a Hugh Evelyn Print

PLATE XI

# The French Court

## Early 15th century

Caprice in fashion can be said to have started in the fourteenth century when, with greater wealth more widely spread, competition in grandeur took place not only between princes and courts but among the newly-rich merchant class trying to dazzle its neighbours and even outstripping the newly-poor nobility who had been systematically reduced in power and wealth by service to kings or the Church. Hitherto, clothes had been mainly functional, growing out of the need for covering and from tradition, with greater richness in material or embroidery to distinguish the lords from their common fellows and with no positive attempt to alter shapes. Even in the early days of chivalry men and women looked very much alike in long flowing robes. The twelfth century introduced a new shape of sleeve and head-dress, but the general style remained static until the new plate-armour made tighter garments necessary and some woman of ideas, noticing their possibilities, had her robe fitted to follow suit and the long-bodied style evolved. There must always have been extrovert characters who wished to be noticed by looking different from the rest, but the opportunities of spreading new fashions were limited while towns were small and the rich were isolated in their castles. The pace of life quickened and society became more gregarious in the fourteenth century when what we now call the rat-race began, with people other than the nobility and their retainers travelling and mixing in the highest circles. The feudal knight had got about a great deal with his interminable wars and Crusades and must have picked up quite a few foreign ideas, but later chivalry, which inclined to sportsmanship rather than learning, made him a poor competitor for the plum jobs of State, in courts and Church, which the able scholar of humble birth (who now formed the professional and patrician class of the community) could attain by a good education. The costly adventures of war had given the merchants and bankers the chance to make fortunes, to travel and offer luxuries from abroad to the grand patrician class as well as to kings and princes. The merchants, in turn, began to vie with the patricians (eventually outstripping them in the social climb) and the craft guilds soon had a larger and better-paying clientele to supply than the old nobility. But even with fierce competition the need remained for a new fashion to be inspired and launched by a well-known and admired personality, and this always appears to have been a member of the aristocracy who had the frivolous leisure for such pursuits, the publicity and the divine right of leadership. This principle held good for centuries, with the notorious taking the place of the aristocrat, until the mid-twentieth century when, in a new wave of socialism and with a stroke of commercial genius, the nondescript and working-class fashion became the ideal. The historical climate has as much influence on appearance as the economic. It is generally the characteristics of the most powerful country that are imitated, in modes and manners, but wars will also create restlessness, a desire for change and a passion for frivolity – and of these the fourteenth century had had its fill. France by virtue of her enterprise had early taken the lead in European affairs and through the culture of her Troubadours had started the way of life, brilliant, cynical and sensual, that has been her characteristic ever since, to the jealous admiration of her neighbours. And France, led by the Queen, at the beginning of the fifteenth century, had the personalities and resources to indulge in frivolities and set fashions. The tall slender Gothic style, introduced and developed by the French, had begun to have its influence on all domestic objects, including dress, which became narrow and elongated, the head-dresses rising and the toes of shoes sprouting long points. Festivity and frivolity have always been expressed in funny hats and it was with these that Queen Isabelle, wife of Charles VI of France and said to be the first real fashion model, put a new look into costume.

Original headgear had begun to make its appearance as women of individuality refused to be eclipsed by uniformity and discovered in the Age of Chivalry how provocative even a veil can be. The tradition that obliged women to cover their hair arose in the first place from the very understandable fear by the Church (voiced by St Paul to the back-sliding Corinthians) of this instrument of sexual temptation, and was accepted in marriage as a sign of submission to the husband who alone had the right to enjoy the wife's natural charms; women married at such an early age that it was only the very young girls who went unveiled. The treatment of their hair until the end of the fourteenth century had inclined to squareness; now the earphones of wire and net that had enclosed the plaits vertically either side of the face under a horizontally hung veil were made to rise up into pointed horns with the veil dipping gracefully between them and floating out at the sides. The head-dresses that men had made from hoods with the *liripipes* twisted round the head now became made-up shapes, called *chaperons*, with large, stuffed rolls as brims and the vestiges of the hood turned into a bag crown or twisted into a coxcomb at one side. Women took over the stuffed rolls in brocade (placing them, at first, in a wide 'U' shape, or tipped up into a point over the forehead, on top of their netted hair) as well as the fine hats blocked in felt or beaver and surmounted by the valuable ostrich feathers introduced by the Saracens from Africa. Men now sported a variety of curled brims or high crowns and tall basin-like caps that became so lastingly popular and, incidentally, served as the foundation of the later steeple head-dresses worn by women.

The decorative but outrageous Isabelle was probably dead before the most extreme fashion, the *hennin* (which is attributed to her) was worn, as there is no pictorial evidence showing these dunces' caps earlier than the 1440s (although a moralising monk is said to have been very outspoken about them in 1428); but it is possible that her own thin hair and lack of eyebrows did inspire the bald and plucked look that is so characteristic of the first half of the fifteenth century. Women suddenly displayed high rounded foreheads under their tipped-back headgear and men underwent the monk-like basin-cut, so short that the head was shaved above the ears and no hair was allowed to sprout on the face – a difficult style to one not blessed with even features, but so well suited to and evocative of the spit-and-polished Henry V and his men at Agincourt.

The line of clothes changed drastically, with great exaggeration in length and width. Belts on women's gowns rose, in the general upward trend, to just under the bosom from which the gored skirts spread, without fullness round the waist or hips, into heavy folds and dragging trains. Necklines were still wide but had begun to dip into a 'V' shape finished, sometimes, with small collars. Although called *houppelandes* like the long, trailing coats of the men, these gowns did not open down the front of the skirt. Robes, for both sexes, were made in rich brocades or velvets and often had the necessary lining of fur (showing at hems or skirt slits) for severe winter wear in draughty castles. High standing collars on men's *jupons*, or under-tunics, showed as a different colour above the collarless *cote-hardis* and were just being sewn to the necks of the short, tunic coats. Sleeves became large and funnel-shaped, flowing from a small shoulder to trail on the ground in extreme designs, but the bag sleeve, gathered into a cuff or band at the wrist and often slit up the front, started its long run of popularity as early as 1400. Dagging, the decoration made by cutting the edges of material at the hems of skirts, sleeves and even hats, all added to the fluttering, festive atmosphere of the period. The carnival spirit was carried even further by borrowing little bells (worn by clowns and flourished at May-Day festivals) and sewing them on to every conceivable part of the dress. A tough constitution was needed to endure the fun and frippery and the oddly contrasted grim pursuits of this period. These ephemeral women spent a great deal of time in the saddle (even riding astride with their skirted legs protected by clumsy leather leggings) hunting wild beasts, and at falconry, which could be more dangerous than it looks, for two queens lost their lives at the sport.

*French Court Dress, c. 1415*

PLATE XII

# The Burgundians

## Early 15th century

By the fifteenth century trade had created a much more complex society whose wealth commanded the refinements of life and allowed it at long last to free itself from the complete domination by the Church. The Christian principle of divine poverty and share-and-share-alike had applied in practice to the already poor or weak and had resulted in an accumulation of wealth at the rather dubious disposal of the Church or feudal lords. Ironically, the greed of kings and the pursuit of the Holy Wars created the merchants and wage-earning craftsmen and labourers who, on the equally excellent principle of making the most of five talents, acquired wealth and defied reprisals from Church or State in their independent towns that had been created by trade. In a materialistic vicious circle, merchants had to handle and accelerate the trade that made the money which kings borrowed to pay for the necessities of the wars to protect the trade. Big business had come to stay and everybody involved moved up a step in the social scale. Little towns of the northern lands grew into important cities as the Hanseatic League (founded, originally, to protect the Baltic trade from local pirates) formed a confederation of commercial cities, able to defend their interests against internal conflict or State interference and offering protection to merchants on their dangerous journeys. Mutual trade made the exchange of personnel essential, however difficult the political situation happened to be between the countries. Merchants of different nations met in foreign cities where they endeavoured to promote trade – and put a spoke into the wheel of their rivals – and their biggest money-spinning commodities had all to do with dress.

The Italians brought silks and brocades, jewellery and armour to northern Europe, while the English were established in France, Flanders and Italy for the sale of their valuable wool and cloth and to purchase furs, felt and fustian (a hard-wearing cotton and linen fabric) from Poland and Germany. The social and political status of a merchant had to be at V.I.P. level, since he had to deal with kings, patricians and burghers in the delicate matters of loans, bills of credit and custom and trade permits. In the pictures we are lucky to

see of them, they appear to have been men of substance and a quiet dignity that comes from a deep experience of life. The portraits came about through the use in art of the Gothic style, a changed attitude to representation and again by the increased number of wealthy lay-patrons, for it is doubtful whether, until this time, a real likeness of a person had been attempted, except perhaps in small miniatures in manuscripts.

The loss of wall space in Gothic churches had caused the art of fresco-painting in Italy to be used less exclusively for religious expression and to blossom on the walls of private houses or public buildings, influenced now by the new humanism and illustrating secular romantic subjects. The even more restricting Gothic of the north constituted a challenge that invoked a different kind of genius, in the new technique of panel-painting and the enjoyment of representing nature. In a totally opposed realisation of an ideal, the southern artist saw man in God and tried to lift him and his surroundings up to sublime heights, while the northern painter found God in man and brought Him down to earth to invest every detail of nature and of daily life with a divine interest. In the latter formula a faithful representation of the object was the goal, which made possible the painting of unidealised portraits. The topmost status symbol of the successful merchant or burgher, and his philanthropy, became the gift of an altar-piece flanked by the portraits of himself and family as donors; and gradually the fancy to have a private likeness of himself in the house made him encourage the Memlings, the Van Eycks, the Bouts and the Van de Weydens to produce the jewel-like pictures of people and everyday scenes that began to appear on the walls of private houses in Flanders and the Netherlands, then all part of the duchy of Burgundy. For it was in this particular part of Europe that the influence in cultural affairs suddenly developed. The French had not been very clever over Burgundy (originally a small province to the south-east and peopled by the descendants of a Germanic barbarian tribe) which had been given in a lordly gesture by Jean le Bon of France to a younger son, as a duchy, in 1364. Marriage alliances – prompted rather short-sightedly by France – the natural talents of its people and the political ability of its rulers (who thought nothing of double-crossing a cousin or nephew), had created a vast territory stretching from the North Sea to Italy and a painful political thorn in the side of France.

For a hundred years Burgundy became a considerable force in Europe, in all but the humanities which found more response from the liberal-minded Italians. In the same way, temperament and climate affected the interpretation of the contemporary art form which we call Gothic, a term coined by the sixteenth century critic and historian, Vasari, in contempt of the barbarian culture that had taken the place of the Classic. Thought and action have always seemed to be more deliberate among the northern people, tending to produce a less flexible means of expression than the more carefree, exuberant south, and, where rules are strict and a very high standard of perfection is the aim, exaggeration to extremes becomes the only means of evolution and variation until a climax is reached and a complete revolution occurs. The vertical ideal of Gothic art was exploited *par excellence* by the rigid Burgundians who, apart from fitting their architecture into the narrowest space possible, pulled out their own extremities to the required slim height by the exaggeration of hats and shoes. The fashionable emaciated look that the Flemish painters portrayed so faithfully was so popular that even the resident foreign merchants in the Netherlands wore it for their portraits to be painted. The typical early fifteenth-century costume worn by Giovanni Arnolfini (an Italian merchant resident in Bruges for forty years) and his wife, as painted by Van Eyck, shows the luxurious details and suitable materials that were worn in Burgundy at this time. As extra protection against the northern climate the sanctimonious Giovanni wears a fur-lined, full tabard over a high-necked tunic. The really prestige part of the attire was the hat that had grown to magnificent proportions by the 1400s. Bruges became the centre for fine hats, where wool and beaver-hair felt was blocked into fat and fantastic shapes by experienced Russian craftsmen who were imported to fashion the top-grade

headgear. Bulbous crowns were narrowed into wide brims, and feathers and garlands completed the grand confection. These wide hats have a curiously extinguishing effect on the high-cropped hair. Hoods ceased to be worn on the head but were pulled down over the shoulders like a small cape. At the other extremity toes of shoes were elongated to add to the impression of height and length. These early 'winkle-pickers' were called *poulaines* by the French and *crakowes* in other parts of Europe, and it is possible that the fashion was brought west by Polish or Bohemian craftsmen working in the Netherlands. Shoes were of such fine leather, or material, that protection was needed against the wet and muddy roads and, so as to preserve their delicacy for indoors, wooden or iron clogs – platform soles with the heels and toes defined – were made to slip on or off easily by a strap over the foot. These quite sensible over-shoes, called *pattens*, later became as fantastic as the shoes, with elongated and upturned toes.

Another typical feature of the period was in the treatment of fullness in tunics and gowns which was pulled down into such sculptured, even folds that it is possible they were sewn on to a lining. Women had raised their waistlines some time ago and had adopted a forward-swinging attitude by lifting the heavy skirt into a bunch in front (much emphasised by Burgundian women) to show a contrasting underskirt. Dagging in intricate cuts at the edges of sleeves and hems was becoming more and more fanciful with one layer of material over another. The merchant's lady in the Van Eyck picture has her bag sleeves decorated with a leafy pattern made from little squares of material, sewn on loosely, in serried rows.

The stuffed-roll *chaperon* with flowing and dagged ends was worn rakishly by both sexes in court circles, but the veil raised on horned cauls above each ear was becoming the most popular head-dress for women in northern countries. The Burgundian and German version edged the veil with layers of crimped or goffered frills.

c. 1430          1434          1434          c. 1430

# Burgundian Dress

Drawn by Faith Jaques © a Hugh Evelyn Print

PLATE XIII

# *Armour*

## *11th to 15th century*

Armour was the most typical costume of the medieval period and deserves a chapter all to itself. The northern people – Franks, Saxons and Norsemen – who became the conquerors of Europe spent so much time in fighting that it is hardly surprising that protective clothing was developed for them (and their mounts), and that the shape of this armour should, later, influence the style of clothes they wore when not in combat. The Scandinavians were probably the earliest Europeans to wear chain-mail as a flexible form of armour, made either by linking iron discs into a mesh or by wiring them on to a leather tunic.

The Danes brought their protective suiting to Britain in the fifth century, and the Norsemen introduced it to France, where it was refined into the lighter-weight chain-mail of closely interlocking small metal rings. The Franks had conquered Gaul from the saddle and very naturally developed cavalry practice as a speciality. And a very expensive business it proved later, as every effort was made to turn man and beast into an animated tank. The horses had to be bred from a heavy but athletic type and trained so that there was no misunderstanding between man and beast in the difficult tactics of charging and manoeuvre. The same applied to the training of knights, to avoid an unfortunate pile-up if the leaders hesitated. No country could afford to bear the cost of this type of army, but by judicious bribery and boosted prestige it could be made to support itself. Charles Martel, the hero of the Franks, made sure of the loyalty and skill of his fighting men by grandly endowing them with estates confiscated from an over-wealthy Church. He, incidentally, had the stirrup perfected so as to give greater mounted stability to his knights.

The earliest armour followed the lines of the everyday clothes of the barbarians, with hooded tunics, or *hawberks*, of chain-mail reaching to below the knees. They were slit up the back and front of the skirts to tie round, inside the leg, for greater comfort in riding. Over the hood a helmet was worn, conical in shape after the Scandinavian pattern and with a stiff piece down the front to protect the nose. Is is interesting to note that in the Bayeux tapestry, dated soon after the Conquest in 1066, the knights are fully covered with chain-mail and armed with spears and heavy battle-axes, but the archers, the good old foot-sloggers who did the most damage to the enemy, were most undemocratically unprotected by chain-mail. A little comfort from the scratching of the mail was allowed the knight by the wearing of a long-sleeved undershirt of linen, leather or wool, by long hose tied round the leg with strips of leather and separate shoes. The next step, in the middle of the twelfth century, was into chain-mail leggings, *chausses* complete with feet, which laced up the back of the leg and were tied to the underbreeches. The *hawberk*, offering greater protection, was now made with long sleeves ending in mittens to protect the hands, and was widened and shortened and often showed the under-tunic below the hem. The *coiffe-de-maille* hood covered the chin and left very little of the face exposed. It appears to have been sufficient protection without a helmet except in heavy action or tournaments. The top of the helm became rounded about 1150, but still had the nasal piece, although this had been found to have distinct disadvantages when the unfortunate King Stephen was taken prisoner in 1141 and led, most humiliatingly, like a bull by the nasal of his helmet. The simple chain-mail suit was satisfactory till the middle of the twelfth century when the strange phenomenon occurred (repeated in history right up to recent years by the young men calling themselves 'Hell's Angels') when the male character was contradicted by its appearance and the brawn and brutality were disguised by trailing robes and flowing hair. The long robe of civilian wear, certainly giving grace and dignity to the figure, then began to be worn *under* the *hawberk*. The girlish look of the knight of early chivalry, who after all was supposed to combine the graces with valour, was probably a cover (like that of the Guards officer, home from Dunkirk in the Second World War, who complained of the noise and the people) for a tough and war-loving character. The long robe had to be slit up the front, and was draped over the back of the horse when mounted. However romantic the glow of these warriors may be in the imagination, the dazzle of the real thing must have been too eye-catching militarily and a nuisance to the 'other ranks', so, about 1200, somebody had the bright idea of wearing a long sleeveless tunic *over* the chain-mail, girt in by a heavy belt which carried the sword. At first the surcoat was of reasonable length but as it was found an ideal ground for armorial bearings it became more ample and again reached to the feet. The prestige and dignity given by these long emblazoned surcoats may account for the downfall in 1370 of the British general, Sir John Chandos (either a showy character or a perfect Blimp as he was wearing a robe that had gone out of fashion years before) who having peevishly challenged a French noble to combat for bearing the same armorial devices as his own, tripped over his long skirts and fell a victim to the death-stroke of his adversary.

The inconvenience of long skirts over prick-spurs (which had been worn since before the Christian era) must have been another reason for shortening the surcoat about the middle of the thirteenth century when it became known as the *cyclas*. This, too, was cut away and slit up the front for convenience by 1300, when the new pieces of plate armour were introduced to reinforce the chain-mail. Pieces of plate shaped to fit the knees, over the chest and up the legs were made in laminated sections, to allow the wearer to move. It is a wonder how any man survived the heat and discomfort of this armour (let alone the vermin) with an under-shirt, a tunic of chain-mail covered by one or more padded tunics over which was the surcoat, with each garment firmly laced and buckled to the other.

Helmets, flat on top in 1200, enclosed the head with slits for breathing and became so large that by the end of the century they rested on the shoulders. In 1300 they became rounded caps, *bascinets*, with hinged visors over the face, and during the century the more comfortable *chapel-de-fer*, resembling the tin-hat of modern warfare, made its appearance. Helms were worn by the mighty and could be crowned by the owner's crest, or symbol, to mark him

out for special notice – a rash policy in battle, one would think. And the horses, too, had their protective mail, hidden under linen covers *barded* with the riders' armorial insignia.

As the practice of making articulated pieces of plate improved and the most effective armour had to fit closely to the limbs, the whole figure became more natural in shape. The thighs as well as the calves of the legs were encased in iron with flexible knee pieces, and by 1360 the loose *cyclas* became the tight jumper-like *jupon* over a metal breast-plate. The new shape, the necessarily tight undergarments and the heavy sword-belt, hanging low on the hips, inspired the civilian fashion for both men and women, and for the former it indicated the long-legged, short-tuniced style that they would wear for a century or more. The *jupons* became *tabards*, sleeved tunics open at both sides and often belted in round the waist with the back left free, which, by the first half of the fifteenth century, covered the top of a complete suit of plate-armour. The plates themselves were sometimes covered in material to prevent rusting and to provide a ground for armorial bearings.

The great helmets were only worn for tournaments in the fifteenth century (a knight even wearing his lady's *hennin* on top of his as a crest) and the retired Italian warriors favoured the great hats of civilian wear for state occasions. Complete suits of plate-armour were made by the fifteenth century but as, by this time, the system of warfare by heavily armoured mounted cavalry was obsolete they must have been used primarily for the nostalgic form of knightly amusement, jousting, that lingered on through the centuries.

The first plate-armour was made in Milan but Germany, too, had perfected the industry and both countries made suits for the English market. The English aristocracy loved their battle dress so dearly that not only the mighty rest in it, in stone, in our churches but that of the lesser fry was engraved most carefully on monumental brasses which are dated, so that it is possible to follow the changes in style through the years.

*Erratum*
*Plate XIII: for* 1150 *read* 1070

c. 1150

1295

1445–1450

1490

## Armour

Drawn by Faith Jaques © a Hugh Evelyn Print

PLATE XIV

# The Italian Courts

## Mid 15th century

The wave of economic prosperity and urbanisation in Europe that raised the standard of living among a greater number of people and brought about more rapidly changing styles in costume had rather a different effect in Italy than elsewhere. To begin with, her social structure was distinct from that of her neighbours in that she was no unified nation under a resident dynasty: the German Holy Roman Emperors had years before given up the struggle to impose their peculiar right of Imperial rule on these unwilling and turbulent people, and the Pope, the only other power, had lost authority through absence abroad. It was therefore a grand free-for-all of one small city-state, or one of the many ambitious classes against another in the race for material power. The maritime cities were the first to rise owing to their wealth of shipping but the inland towns advanced as the demand for luxury goods grew with the enhanced spending powers of certain members of the community. With commercial rights to uphold – and purloin, property to protect – and confiscate, the constant poaching on each other's preserves fostered the enmity that kept towns fortified and always on the alert. The constant warfare bred the *condottieri*, those most unideal knights, or military leaders, who made a business out of fighting for the highest bidder and, by careful manipulation of the protection racket as much as by honest fighting, were able to join the ranks of the rulers and establish themselves in some instances, such as Este in Ferrara and Sforza in Milan, as Dukes of States. Here in Italy, as elsewhere, society turned topsy-turvy, but whereas in England younger sons took to trade and repaired the family fortunes, or successful merchants bought themselves lordships of manors without aspiring to the nobility, the patrician or wealthy merchant in Italy bought out the old hereditary nobles or allowed them to marry into their families at the price of their estates and often their titles. Agriculture being as important as ever to keep the growing community fed, the landed nobles either had to borrow money for their estates or go into trade themselves. Many migrated to the cities, as is evident by the wealth of small palaces and villas in every Italian town and all the stories of family feuds that have gone down in popular romance. Feudal as society had been before, it did not become democratic by the change-over; with everyone scrambling for titles and positions of importance, the ruling class became an aristocracy of money. This meant a proliferation of small courts, refurbished old ones and many newly-rich, with palaces in towns and villas and castles in the countryside where the competition in splendour could be carried out in style.

The commercial spirit was so strongly ingrained in the middle-class Italian that family wealth endured through several generations, in spite of extravagance, and not only the founders but the younger sons could enjoy a leisured existence and had the opportunity to indulge their personal inclinations and taste in urbane and luxurious living. And by a miracle, the old nobles and the upstarts all seemed to have possessed an unerring standard of taste in the fine arts, which it became the fashion to enjoy, however lacking in virtue the rest of their behaviour may have been. At least there was competition in patronage and the encouragement brought forth the artistic genius that abounded in the Italian states in the fifteenth century. The cult of humanism, too, which put a value on civilised manners, counterbalanced both the vulgarity and the affectation to nobility suffered by a monied élite by maintaining the necessity for artists and scholars to play an important part in cultured society. But here, as elsewhere in Europe at the time, the precariousness of life and the ever-present probability of unpleasant death through plague, revenge or war was reflected in a swinging, eating, drinking and merry-making society and its rapidly changing and fantastic fashions. Harking back to romance, all the nonsense of chivalry, tournaments and high-society play-acting were revived in the courts of Milan, Ferrara and Mantua where fashion became fancy-dress.

The Gothic ideal in costume, as in architecture in Italy, did not stray so far from the oriental original as was the case in the frigid north. There is a blandness and rounded sumptuousness about the exaggeration of detail directly contrary to the angular Burgundian or French styles, although so many of the fundamental ideas were the same. Emphasis was put on height but it was rarely pointed; folds were made to conform to a sculptured pattern but the figures they covered were never emaciated, and bands of fur, embroidery or heavy fringes took the place of the ragged dagging so dearly loved by the Germanic people. In fact, the Italian idea was to clothe a normal figure, however fantastically; not to design a fashion into which the pliable human frame had to fit. The romantic appeal of trailing skirts and sleeves and of mounting hair styles was taken to the ultimate extreme by the Italians, up to the middle of the fifteenth century. With money no object, yards of the most expensive material were put into women's gowns that were cut almost circularly and gathered into neck bands, or little yokes, to give enormous fullness to long-trained skirts. The great width was pulled together into even pleats at a small high waist but the shape of the figure was almost obliterated by the huge bat-wing sleeves, also cut from circles and gathered into the armholes of the gown. These, heavily bordered and often of more than one layer of material, hung over the arms and trailed away into the skirt, or were turned back, cape-like, and folded on the shoulders to show a contrasting lining of brocade or fur. Older men wore the same trailing *houppelande*, but open down the front, and the younger men now wore knee-length tunics, cut similarly with the fluted pleats splaying out like a parasol to a fur-bordered hem, or held in very tightly at a normal waist-line. It was in the design of sleeves that the Italians really let themselves go. Of the same length as the tunic and circularly cut, they were set into the shoulders by formal pleats and were either slit up the front, like capes, or turned back in wide folds on one or both shoulders. Another fancy idea was to make them elbow-length in front, with a wide border of fur dipping to the hem of the tunic at the back.

The gowns and tunics of both sexes were modestly high-necked in front but had a tendency, probably due to the weight of the material, to slope away at the back, revealing the small standing collar of the doublet which was often finished by a tiny white 'tucker'. The high necklines on the women's gowns were even emphasised by choker necklaces. The bald look so popular in other parts of Europe was effected in Italy by severe hairdressing, with the front hair strained off the forehead but piled up into great turbans of twisted rolls or plaits, far back on the crown of the head. Melon-shaped caps were worn by those not so gifted by nature. Trying and uncomfortable as these styles must have been, the highbrow look did give the wearer an air of distinction – a fact that did not escape the designers of the class-levelling fashions of the 1960s when they perpetrated the Beatle hair-cut. The severe bowl-cut for men was gradually giving way to a still short but puffed-out style which showed in curls under the enormous headgear. Huge turban-like *chaperons* had bag crowns, and the popular beaver hat, also fur-edged, was blocked with a domed crown and Breton-sailor brim, to be cocked at the wearer's fancy.

The constant thirst for entertainment made the resident 'funny men' essential to medieval courts. Their costume followed the line of current fashion, emphasising the most piquant details, but retained the old peaked hood with bells and the parti-colour that was fast becoming the livery of servants. The exaggerated styles of this period were obviously the wear of the leasured rich, but judging by the number of sumptuary laws that were passed in the vain hope of keeping a distinction of rank by dress, there must have been many social climbers able to copy and even outdo the fashion of their betters.

c. 1440                                    1440–1450                                    c. 1480

# Italian Court Dress

PLATE XV

## English and Flemish Peasants

❧⁓✦⁓❧

## Mid 15th century

The working people of England and Burgundy (which included Flanders and the Netherlands) in the mid fifteenth century were rather better off than their predecessors or their neighbours for quite contrary reasons but had many other things in common. In England the people had won a democratic victory, feudalism and serfdom were rapidly dying out, and quite fortuitously through the grim toll taken by continuing bouts of plague and war the labourer gained his most valuable weapon against exploitation – the power to bargain for decent wages owing to a shortage of labour. The noble landowner, who was finding it difficult to make both ends meet through the high cost of hired labour, became a landlord as he was forced to let his property in farms to the thrifty and ambitious peasants who had risen by work and ability above their fellows. A system of communal farming was also tried out, by peasant cultivators joining their strips of common land, and everybody who could, kept sheep.

While the nobles, with affiliations to the cause of either Red or White Rose, were tearing themselves and their traditions to pieces in the race for the throne or the power behind it, the rest of their countrymen appear, from a contemporary account, to have placidly continued going about their daily job of producing food and clothing for the rest of the community. The great estates, not necessarily baronial but also the manors of the yeomen gentry, were self-contained industrial communities where food was grown and prepared and all the stages of cloth production and the making of household goods were undertaken by craftsmen living in their cottage homes. The lady of the manor conducted the same occupation on a smaller scale for her household, adding to it the organisation of family affairs and often the administration of the estate with one eye on the well-being of her tenants and work-people – which may account for the close resemblance between many of the ladies on memorial church brasses and the modern efficient committee woman. Quite unco-operative in the matter of contributing to national taxes, and if able to pay his rent or in the employment of a good landlord, the English agricultural worker

had never had it so good.

The Burgundian, on the other hand, in the reign of Philip the Good, was still living under an almost Feudal system, for the simple reason that the wily Duke (the only able ruler in Europe at the time) strengthened his own position by a show of great wealth and all the extravagances of a court the other dim and impoverished rulers could no longer afford. He retained at great cost the out-dated exercises of nobility and chivalry as a sop to his nobles and became, as an example, a great patron of the arts, with the result that there was a steady and increasing demand for and output of high quality luxury goods for the home and eager foreign markets and plenty of work for the agricultural labourer to support the industrial community. A great English lady, Margaret of York, sister to King Edward IV, had married Charles, the son of the Duke of Burgundy, which probably made the traffic between the two countries more frequent. The acquaintance of the people of the Netherlands by English soldiers during the Hundred Years War (when Burgundy was occasionally on our side) and the business dealings of English merchants for many generations must have strengthened the similarities between the two countries in spite of continued strained relations politically. Agricultural life in both countries must have been very much the same, as no revolutionary ideas had disturbed the method of ploughing or reaping and, although the commercial side of the production of cloth (of prime importance to both peoples) had become accelerated, the processes and keeping of sheep had not changed. There must also have been similarities in the countryside, especially in the eastern counties of England where much new building was in brick – an idea picked up from Flanders and now become indigenous as it saved the transport of heavy building material to stoneless counties and preserved scarce timber for interior work.

In one important matter the English lagged far behind their Flemish neighbours: though highly skilled and observant in the art of illustration, they appear to have been quite unaware of picture painting, which merchants and soldiers must have seen but not noticed in their long sojourns in the Netherlands where local painters held exalted rank – such as Van Eyck as Gentleman of the Bedchamber to Philip of Burgundy – and, praise be, made an excellent living from their wealthy patrons in court, State and commercial circles. For this reason we have little idea what our medieval ancestors looked like and why an attempt has been made to invoke a picture of them from the culture of the people nearest to them at a time (one of many) when there was a close contact between the two nations.

The general prosperity is very well reflected in the clothes of the peasants illustrated in the miniature pictures of the innumerable Books of Hours created at this time. The general tendency in men's costume was to tighten and creep upwards, following the Italian influence of a Classical display of limbs, which meant that leg-covering had to be longer and better-fitting. The ordinary individual of any country had no idea, of course, what had inspired a fashion in the absence of popular communication on the subject such as we have now, but followed the style of his betters who had copied a fashion that looked good on some admired personality – and it is astonishing how quickly novel ideas were accepted and put into general effect. It is also a maxim that the effect of a novel idea has always come before comfort, so well illustrated by the hose and their fastening at this period. With no knitted or expanding material or easy methods of fastening at their disposal tailors had to fit the hose closely to the leg either by cutting the material on the cross or by using a very springy quality, and it is not surprising that country-made garments look a bit clumsy. Before a real effort was made to fashion the breeches and hose all in one piece the latter only reached to the thighs like long stockings. The shaping of two pieces to be sewn together to cover the legs and the behind, allowing for room to bend and sit down, seems to have eluded experienced cutters for a long time. The hose had to be held up as the material did not cling and the only method used for so long was by tying them to the edge of the under-tunic with laces, called points. Underdrawers or,

in the frequent absence of these, shirts, were tucked into the wide tops of the hose with an effect that was hardly satisfactory or comfortable. Those in high fashion were still wearing the *cote-hardi*, long enough to cover the untidy gap, but among the working people where such finesse was of no importance and tunics had sometimes to be cut according to the cloth the shirt was frankly allowed to hang out or the underdrawers to show. Over-stockings or long-legged boots with leather soles were beginning to be worn for rough work or riding. These had to be loose for the foot to enter easily and were either tied round the knees with thongs or appear to be in danger of falling down. The *cote-hardi* became close-fitting and was rapidly becoming the jerkin or jacket worn over the under-tunic or doublet. The poorer people would only have been able to afford one of these garments over a shirt which generally showed above the collarless neck of the jerkin whose fullness would naturally have none of the nicety of pleats or gathers of the fashionable garment being very homespun and home-made. Men's hats, however, were both practical and varied, made in fur or felt with ear-flaps to tie under the chin or over the top in Sherlock Holmes style. The wearing of hoods persisted among the working class until late in the century.

Where the shape of a woman's gown cut in one piece with a small top and wide swing was too difficult or too expensive to follow, the bodice was cut separately, and straight pieces gathered into the waist made the wide skirt – in the most enduring of female fashions. The simple opening down the front of the bodice was also the forerunner of many later fashions with its lacing across a shift or kirtle. Detachable sleeves were another thrifty and practical idea enabling a change to be made according to the weather or the importance of an occasion. The custom of covering the hair with cunningly draped veils and wimples was very much a Burgundian, Flemish tradition, but for work in the fields the peasant woman would have tied up a kerchief into a modest mob cap.

*English and Flemish Peasant Dress, 1460*

PLATE XVI

# The French and Flemish

## Mid 15th century

After their tutelage by Italy, the countries of a particular area of western Europe – England, eastern France, the Netherlands and western Germany – founded an enduring centre of commerce and enjoyed the effects of a steady increase in big business and capitalism resulting in better conditions for the many and the usual display on the part of their wealthier citizens. The main source of this prosperity was still the wool trade which had so astonishingly enabled England not only to enter the community at an early stage but later to wreck the economy of her rivals so successfully that they were forced to develop other industries. The Netherlands, once the most important centre for fine woollen cloth, were in the mid-fifteenth century starved of English wool, the suppliers having found the Italians a better market as they shipped their own imports, but also because the English were now producing fine cloth themselves and needed more of their own good wool. English cloth had gained such a reputation in its short history that it was valued for its appearance, its wearing and weather-proof qualities and apparent cheapness, for it was said that 'all sorts, from the highest to the lowest are cloathed wherewith', and still there was enough to export overseas. The worsted, called after the Norfolk village where it was first made, was as fine as silk and so much sought after that customers were willing to wait months for the delivery of enough material to make a smart tunic, we hear from the *Paston Letters*. Whether the English were merely tactless or short-sighted we shall never know, but certainly theirs was shabby and slighting treatment of the Flemish wool merchants and Duke Philip the Good who had flatteringly instituted the Order of the Golden Fleece (second only to the most noble European knighthood, the Order of the Garter) in honour of the English staple situated at that time at Antwerp, which brought such riches into the Duchy of Burgundy. The fullers and weavers of Bruges, Ghent and Ypres (towns always in the front line of economic or political warfare) were the greatest sufferers, being reduced to destitution and emigration, even to England, but the astute businessmen of the Netherlands found other lines

of the textile trade with which to make up for the loss of the cloth market. Spanish wool, vastly inferior to the English in quality but cheap and plentiful, made inexpensive clothing material, and linen of an incredible fineness, the 'cambric' of Cambrai, was perfected to fashion the lovely head-dresses, wimples and underlinen that began to play a greater part in the costume of the respectable world.

Although building methods had improved and glass now filled lattice windows (the craft was established in Flanders by Duke Philip in 1453), tiled floors and stone walls made the atmosphere far from cosy, accounting for the popularity of fur-lined garments and the heavy curtains and screening in living rooms. The grand families had material-hung walls, often with a pattern made from personal devices woven into the fabric, which developed into the fashion for whole pictures to be woven to fill a wall space. For some reason there has always been a little confusion over tapestry. The weaving method, which was hard and employed several workers simultaneously, was copied from that used in Persia for rugs and hangings and was not developed from lady-like embroidery, and the name tapestry was derived from an old one given to coarse material, not a floor covering. As the skill developed, famous artists were commissioned to design the woven pictures as they had the previous wall paintings, and Flanders, with Arras as the centre, became the unsurpassed district of the tapestry industry, weaving having been established there for ten centuries owing to the plentiful supply of madder and other dye-stuffs. Even the designs of Raphael were sent to Arras to be woven, and although other towns competed with it in production, such as Tournai and Gobelins, the name 'Arras' became used as the generic term for all tapestry – as we hear from the unpleasant fate of the unfortunate Polonius. The purchasers of fifteenth-century tapestry had a peculiar liking for contemporary scenes with figures dressed in the high fashion, which can be checked against the many portraits and miniatures made and dated at this time. It was only in a wealthy productive area that clothes could have become so rich in material and design and although France was in a poor state, politically, from the fourteenth century her rulers managed to do themselves proud in Paris, on heavily imposed taxes, and the court of Burgundy provided an example of sartorial excellence and extravagance that the large and rich middle class was quick to imitate. The early tapestries of Flemish design, like the ones on which our figures are based, naturally showed an idealised fashion, like a modern fashion-plate, but they did reflect the nature and circumstances of the people. Conservatively clinging to the remnants of nobility, or aspiring to it, their clothes have almost reached the peak of romantic exaggeration but their wearers have such a look of cool elegance that they are saved from vulgarity or absurdity.

The change in style from the French to the Burgundian-influenced, narrow silhouette can be seen in the women's garments which changed from the flowing-sleeved *houppelandes* to the gowns whose bodices were cut separately from the skirts so as to preserve a small flat top. The necessary fullness of the gored skirt was pleated rigidly into a high, tight waist accentuated by a wide, stiff belt which often had a completely modern buckle, eyelets and tags. The neckline, outlined by a turned-back collar, swooped down in a deep 'V' to the waistline, showing a 'modesty front' of the kirtle underneath. Heavy collar-necklaces filled in the opening of the dress as a very typical detail of the period. Sleeves that had been trailing or bag-shaped became long and tight-fitting and darted on the shoulders to give the fashionable angular shape.

The plucked-brow look had reached a stage of baldness as the hair was completely concealed in a wired-net caul and decorated with a dipping, stuffed roll, or by a stiff conical cap under the magnificently folded and wired cambric veils. These were secured to the coif, or cap, by decorative pins – a novelty at the period but obviously very popular, with the heads formed like naturalistic insects that appear to have alighted on the veil. The small crescent on the forehead may have been a tab for pulling the *hennin*

from slipping off the back of the head. There also appears to have been a class distinction about these head-dresses. The great ladies wore theirs perched above the ears while the burgesses were inclined to let the ends drop more primly on to the shoulders, in a nun-like fashion.

Men's clothes altered more gradually in the north, the Burgundians being conservative and apt to drag out a fashion to its ultimate extreme. The tunic, with a high collar, was becoming shorter by the mid-fifteenth century and, fastened by hooks instead of rows of buttons and with the skirts cut separately from the top to ensure a wide flare, was very much more of a jacket or jerkin than previous garments. The under-tunic or doublet of a contrasting colour still had a high standing collar but became shorter and tighter to carry the longer hose. Padding was put across the chest and top of the arm to emphasise the fashionable narrow body line and small waist. There is no wonder that the older men and officials clung to their long skirted *houppelandes* as the jackets became embarrassingly shorter; the pleats of the long garment, however, were made to follow the fashionable line, pulled in to the centre of the waist. Heavy belts carried the important purse and short dagger of the rich burgher. Sleeves were not as tight as those of women's gowns and were pleated in to the armhole and often slit from shoulder to wrist to show the material of the under-tunic. The *chaperon* had become a completely made-up hat with a roll brim and a conventionalised hood with long ends sewn to it to be draped this way or that.

Both sexes wore wonderful Venetian or Genoese brocades of silk, or silk and velvet, in a large diaper pattern; yellow, once the sign of Jews, had now become a very popular colour.

c. 1450            1450-1475            1450-1475            1480

# Franco-Flemish Dress

Drawn by Faith Jaques © a Hugh Evelyn Print

PLATE XVII

# The Burgundian Court

## Late 15th century

The rulers of Burgundy had become so successful and powerful in the fifteenth century that they were apt to forget they were Princes of France and behaved as despots of an independent State, which to all intents and purposes they were, as their riches far exceeded those of France and the Duke was king in all but name. Philip, still alive and crafty in 1460, had modelled his court on those of the fabulous tales of chivalry so as to keep his nobles happy and ready for the defence of the realm, and to impress upon his neighbours the wealth and importance of Burgundy. To uphold the prestige of nobility a ritual of behaviour, corresponding to etiquette, became the rule, making the chosen few even more exclusive than the knights of the early Middle Ages. There was an expensive passion for the tournament which displayed the nobles to advantage as members of a chosen race, and as during the lifetime of Duke Philip Burgundy had been kept comparatively peaceful, it acted as a steam valve for their energies. In maintaining the prestige of nobility the Duke ensured his own exclusive position by making his nobles into courtiers and dependent on the royal patronage – a heavy price had to be paid in submission for the glory of knighthood. At no other court was the etiquette so rigid. There were still only knives to eat with and these probably had to be shared, but the enormous dinner was served by young knights and squires suffering their apprenticeship as courtiers, and every noble was given the respectful treatment due to his rank. The whole set-up bore the mark of the Duke's personality; austere, narrow and affected but with impeccable taste and a love for beautiful objects – a temperament which the costume of the time reflected to perfection. The Duke, himself, may be reckoned as a very important fashion-setter. It was not only the extreme exaggeration of shape for which the Burgundian court was the model: Philip knew how to make a dramatic effect, by appearing himself all in black against his colourful nobles or, on an official visit, startling the company by attending with a retinue completely clad in black. It is thought that he encouraged the use of this colour as the finest local cloth came up best in black, but credit should be given to his original taste and knack of being outstanding. The elegance and distinction of black was recognised from this time, more especially by the descendants of the Burgundian Dukes, the Spanish royal family who exploited it so cunningly in their much imitated costume of the early sixteenth century. Contact with the Italians by commerce must have made their classically inspired costume familiar to the people of northern Europe, but the upward urge of the design in Burgundian clothes had its inspiration in the Perpendicular image of Gothic architecture. Putting the two theories into practice in Burgundy gave costume rather a different effect. The natural figure was not admired to the same extent in the north, or perhaps it failed to come up to the accepted standard, and a good deal of bombasting and reinforcing was thought necessary to gain the ideal line of broad shoulders, small waist and tapering hips. The original idea was quite overlooked in the enthusiasm that produced some dumbfounding results. The shortness of men's tunics, however, did provoke a chorus of protests and abuse to the effect that it was possible to see a man's anatomy as well as his underpants. Recognising the strength of the argument, somebody must have turned his earnest attention to the problem of cutting the hose in one piece, as a form of tights can be seen on figures of workmen not wearing the concealing jackets. They were woefully tight and still without sufficient room in the seat, so that the laces, or points, tying them to the doublet (now given the explanatory name of *pourpoint*) had to be loosened while doing a strenuous job. From a study of drawings of the masters, and in particular those of Dürer (which were less inclined to idealise mundane details), it would appear that the first full hose were made like long stockings cut slanting at the top with the inner edge only reaching to the crutch but the outer as high as the waist and often tucked into a belt. This still left a wide 'V' shape of shirt or pants and needed a flap over the front to preserve decency. The next step was to join the two legs, providing enough space for sitting while avoiding a bloomer effect round the front. Even this was at last achieved in spite of the lack of elastic material, so great was the desire to wear even shorter tunics – but at the cost of putting all the young men back into the discomfort of armour. The doublets were not always cut in two parts but the cartridge pleats were so evenly pulled in at the waist to accentuate the wide shoulder-line that they seem to have been cut separately and laid on to the garment from the shoulder seams or a small yoke. The high stiff collar of the doublet stood above the round neckline of the jacket, usually trimmed with a band of fur which dipped into a point at the back and finely set off the popular chain collar, lying flat over the shoulders and following the shape of the neckline at the back. Sleeves were gathered into the armholes with as many as six darts to ensure a flat, horizontal fullness, but were either straight and long, so that they could be pulled up the arm into creases, or loose-hanging with a slit to allow the doubleted arm to pass through.

The pointed shoes were a direct counterpart to the tall *hennins* and equally cranky, but just as the long finger-nails and cramped toes of Chinese women marked the degree or circumstances of the wearer, and since reasoned criticism creates cussedness, the fashion lasted for over a century. So outrageous had the length become that sumptuary laws were passed against them by both Charles VI of France and Edward IV of England who sought to keep the fashion exclusive by regulating the points according to the rank of the wearer. In England anybody under the rank of baron had to restrict the 'beak' to one foot in length, 'under pain of cursing by the clergy' (which would hardly have been likely to deter the really fashion-conscious) and a fine of twenty shillings by Parliament for every pair – which was found to be much more restraining. It has been recorded that through the difficulty in walking the extra long points were tied up to the knees of the wearer by fine chains, but careful research has failed to find pictorial evidence of this. So dearly was this fashion loved that it was even copied in armour, and the sad fate of the Austrian knights at Sempach in 1366 who, forced to fight on foot, were firmly fixed in the mud by their spiked feet, did nothing to stop the evolution of the fashion.

The change in hair styles was most marked. From a bowl-cut of the early part of the century the hair was allowed to grow to chin length, dipping at the back, and was curled and puffed out over the ears from a centre parting. Real hats, blocked like bowlers, replaced the *chaperon*, and tall caps were perched like egg-cosies on bobbed, wavy hair. The dunce's cap *hennin* seems to have been the brainchild of Burgundian women. Covered in brocade or embroidered with the wearer's monogram it rested insecurely on the head, above the ears, with a long veil suspended from the point hanging down behind but softening the hard line over the forehead. Constant difficulty in keeping it steady prompted the idea to edge it with a band or to copy the humbler woman's hood on which to mount it, turning back the edge to fall close to the ears and on to the shoulders. The gown was at its extreme of length and tightness with a wide high belt and close-fitting sleeves projecting over the hands. The sharp *décolleté* began to spread sideways in a bot shape edged with a bertha collar and showing a wide 'modesty' of the kirtle, but it could be filled in with a contrasting colour to show off the beautiful collar-necklace. The gored skirts were so long that the noble lady needed a train-bearer and her less important sister developed the typical female attitude of the period by swaying forward in walking or clutching her skirts in a bundle over her stomach.

*Burgundian Court Dress, 1480-1500*

Drawn by Faith Jaques © a Hugh Evelyn Print

PLATE XVIII

# The Italian Renaissance

## Late 15th century

The City States of Italy had settled down in the mid-fifteenth century to a steady economic and cultural progress under a younger generation of the independent rulers, merchants, industrialists and adventurers who had established a material society founded on competition and initiative and were busy spending the money so industriously collected by their forebears. In Burgundy the cultural influence of the Dukes and the court was apparent in the creative art of the provinces whereas in Italy the proliferation of small courts and original personalities, all competing for prestige, gave a challenge for a great diversity of ideas. There was no unity of law or constitution in fragmented Italy and the behaviour of some arrogant individuals appears to have been unspeakable, yet the heritage that has been handed down to us conveys an impression of people with some lofty ideas and the skill and industry to achieve them.

It has been said that there has rarely been a time when the opportunities of self-expression were so unrestrained as among the rich families of Italy, and although some natures were better left unexpressed, many others passed on the liberal gift to scholars and artists enabling them to contribute to the common cultural revolution and wealth. The concept of patronage was rather different from the kind with which we are painfully familiar. Money was not spent or encouragement given as an investment or a private personal gratification. Although family palaces were built they went to enhance the beauty of the town that had benefitted equally from the Ducal bounty and local talent was encouraged from motives of civic pride and display. The patrons were lucky in that they do not appear to have had the difficulty of selection facing unfortunate town-councillors under the present system of State patronage and the new concept of individuality.

As exciting as the encouragement of the new was the passion for the antique, awakened by the study of Classical philosophy. The search for inscriptions led to a fresh appreciation of architecture and sculpture and, we regret to say, a fair number of fakes and improvements on the genuine article.

All parties appear to have been pleased by this arrangement, the forger being given credit for his scholarship and skill and the savants quite satisfied to be taken in as long as there was new and exciting material to discuss. Long journeys in search of fresh Classical treasures were undertaken by earnest scholars who were ready to oblige with quite delightful but bogus accounts and sketches of their finds to satisfy the popular demand at home. So deeply steeped in mythology was one scholar that he invoked Mercury as a safeguard before setting out on a hazardous journey. The antiquarian fever did at least save from further decay or deterioration some of the ruins and sculptured objects lying on their own doorstep to be handed down as the few survivors of the glory that was Greek or Roman.

Literature did not escape the enthusiasts with their curious medieval-cum-mythical romances, foreshadowing a later outbreak of obsession with the antique – the Gothic revival of ruins and romance – in another period of material success. The important thing is that the new tendency not only engaged the interest of the talented artists of the time in Florence, Urbino and Mantua, but positively made them, as they rose to the challenge of creation on the grand scale. Botticelli, Cosimo Tura and Pinturicchio were particularly receptive of the Classical idea and it is difficult to know if they were not carried away by their inventive genius or if the delightful costume worn by the figures in their compositions approximates in any way to the clothes worn at the time. One thing is certain, that the conception of Classical costume did loosen the style of fashion from the rigid Burgundian influence to a broader and more flowing line – even if it did go through a few contortions on the way. Another characteristic of the new influence was that the shortening of garments and lengthening of hair did give an air of perennial youth to the people of the late fifteenth century.

The figure on the right of Plate XVIII shows the style of dress most common until 1480 when still under the powerful influence of Burgundy – men's tunics fitted with a rigid arrangement of cartridge pleats set into a yoke to control the otherwise very full garment. Fashionable and well-cut clothes now had doublets reaching to the hips to support the hose that were increasingly made like tights. Tabard tunics, a very youthful fashion since it is generally associated with early heralds, were worn to cover the still untidy line of the join of doublet and hose. Shoes, never so exaggerated in Italy as elsewhere, had become a graceful and natural fit with a medium point. The tall Burgundian caps that had originally been worn under large hats or *chaperons* were fashionable in Italy until 1476 when Charles the Bold finally got his deserts at the battle of Grandon and the power and influence of Burgundy was broken for good.

The costume that then developed was obviously thought up by the artistic young bloods of Florence and was very definitely based on the Classical appreciation of the natural form. Hose were brought up to the waist and to avoid creases the tops were cut like shorts and decorated in stripes or chequered patterns. Their tight fit had made the flap or cod-piece now very necessary. Parti-colour hose had had a long popularity and here they had their last appearance – quite uninfluenced by the Classical trend. Half-boots indicated the traveller as shoes were still rather delicate in make, showing the shape of the foot. The doublet shrank to the waist and began to have a wider neckline showing the shirt over the top, instead of the neat standing collar of the previous fashion. Another detail that was to become the characteristic style of the next century was the treatment of detachable sleeves which began as early as 1460. The shirt was now allowed to puff through the opening at the shoulder where the sleeve was caught to the doublet by fancy laces, often placed in groups. The fashion for catching the open sleeve seam at intervals down the arm and letting the shirt puff through could also have been prompted by the method of fastening a Greek *chiton* over the arms, so far does the practice stray from the inspiration in costume design.

In the fine abandon of a freer way of life the hair was allowed to touch the shoulders in long ringlets which balanced a tiny cap in page-boy style, and no beards, as yet, were allowed to spoil the youthful appearance.

Children appear more in Italian pictures than in those of Burgundy or France at this time and the sensitivity with which they are portrayed gives the feeling that they were as loved and spoilt as they are today. They wore miniature replicas of adult clothes with long tights tied up to tiny doublets in the same complicated method as their fathers had to endure. Even the sleeves were in two parts laced together. The tabard tunic is here left free of a belt, as became the adult fashion in the last years of the century.

1500                             *c. 1480*                      *1465-1470*                  *1470*

# *Italian Renaissance Dress*

PLATE XIX

# The Italian High Renaissance

## Late 15th century

We know that time and circumstance must be favourable to the rise of individuality and talent, but that so much genius should have been simmering in Italy in the fifteenth century appears to be a miraculous coincidence. It is impossible to think of the Renaissance in Europe without speaking of the Medicis, for of all the gifted personalities that blossomed at that time and put a spur to the talent of others none was more influential than the several generations of the Medici family. From a simple beginning as merchants and, as the family fortune expanded, money lenders, the Medici family developed an astonishingly versatile bent towards diplomacy, philanthropy, scientific research, artistic ability and taste as well as adding to their fortunes as international bankers by financing heads of state in the expenses of war or keeping out of war. As patrons they were not too interfering, urging, perhaps, a little restraint in the matter of cherubim to the painter Gozzoli, but accepting a design for a building outright or rejecting it completely sooner than expect an architect to modify his ideas. Some were more than gifted amateurs; if modern scholarship is correct a few buildings around Florence may have been the conception of Cosimo, and Lorenzo was an author and poet of no mean reputation. In all the expenditure of keeping up the magnificence there are no stories of spending for the sake of impressing, unlike the banquet at a later date, served by the merchant Agostimo Chigi on gold plate that was thrown out of the windows with the left-overs into the Tiber at the end of each course. In fact the source of their wealth, usury, was an indigestible weight on the consciences of the older Medici who did endeavour to spend much of it in social benefits. That it should be used to the best advantage reflects the mind of the careful business man, Cosimo, who is quoted as saying, 'Only have patience with me, my Lord, and I will return it all to you.' The same spirit of appreciation of the benefits of comfort and beauty distinguishes so many of the leading personalities of the Renaissance in Italy – from self made families but, as portrayed by their artistic fellow-citizens, people of an aloof dignity reflecting a high standard of taste and behaviour, in contrast to the rugged

donors of Flemish paintings or the German grandees of the sixteenth century.

The fame of Florence and the Medicis was spread by her fabulous merchandise and their agents, particularly those in Burgundy where one, Tommaso Portinari, imitated his master's line of patronage and princely living so lavishly that it unfortunately ruined the Medici bank in Bruges. Posterity can condone this lapse as it did produce the wonderful Van der Goes altarpiece now in the Uffizi which, incidentally, shows Maria Portinari in the finest example of Burgundian fashion – as a compliment perhaps to the Flemish. Florence became the centre of culture at the fall of Constantinople in 1453 and the subsequent decline in the fortunes of her rival Venice, as many refugee scholars with much of the wisdom of the East in manuscript took refuge there and were protected by the Medici. But life was not entirely smooth for the family, and Florence, having found them too overbearing, at the end of the fifteenth century banished them for a matter of eighteen years. Perhaps it is not too risky to suggest that the sudden blossoming of artistic talent in Venice, the place of exile, may have been due to the encouraging presence of the Medici. Not one of this otherwise imaginative family can be said to have been a figure of fashion – the majority were rather ill-favoured and inclined towards simplicity in dress – but their wide interest in the arts, as well as creating the opportunity for young artists to flourish, made the atmosphere congenial to a movement of ideas. It is possible that with an enhanced status the said artists launched the sort of costume we see in their paintings. As Dürer in Germany (but after a trip to Italy) undoubtedly rather fancied himself in the new advanced styles, a preoccupation with clothes can be seen in the work of Carpaccio, Signorelli and Pinturicchio.

Nowhere else in Europe was so much importance attached to dress as in Italy, as suitable attire was felt to complete the perfect figure of a man. Earlier in the century a contemporary said that there was no prevailing fashion in Florence as it had so many talented individualists and exponents. Clothes under the Classical influence had been growing looser and wider in

Italy but the aim of the exercise was rather defeated by the type of material that Florence and Genoa continued to produce so sumptuously. The heavy brocades and velvets did not drape and cling to the figure as the thin linens and wool of ancient Greece had done, and the nymphs of Botticelli were either clothed in imported muslins from Flanders or in the artist's ready imagination. The combination of Classic theory and medieval upholstery did, however, produce something most attractive and original. Italy being usually so warm for much of the year, the high doublet collars were never popular and when someone threw his jacket open and turned down the collar it was an instant success. The wider line suggested the idea of discarding the belt and loosening the pleats, so that the tunic could hang free and almost square on the figure. The lapels and wide collar were now the focal point of the design and treated accordingly with fur or contrasting materials. The hose were better cut, reaching right up to the waist where they were tied by laces with fancy tags. Some doublets were long enough to hang over the waistline or had a small, becoming basque added, in which case the points were tied underneath. Turned-back collars showed the vest and introduced the fine smocked or embroidered shirts that filled the opening of the doublet which was fastened by crossed lacing. Sleeves were more interesting, with puffs of shirt showing at the shoulders and elbow and even the seams caught together by fancy lacing. The popularity of detachable pieces of garments and so much puffing did not detract from a good silhouette as the wearers were either young and slim or had the sense to cover themselves in the alternative fashion of the long gowns that were the *houppelandes* of yesteryear brought up to date with long creased-up sleeves and wide revers. The loose robes were the sole legacy of medieval dress that continued unabashed into the next century as comfortable and dignified wear for the elderly and as academic or civic dress.

The independent social attitude of the time combined with Classicism brought out the long hair styles, now reaching the shoulder in ringlets or curled under in a roll to the nape of the neck. Small pillbox caps began to be decorated with fancy clips and often a single feather. The heavy material may have helped to dictate the change in shape of women's gowns which became almost even in length all round and lost the heavy dragging trains. If the dress had to be lifted it was held up in front but much less in Italy than in the northern countries where the stance of the figure became more exaggerated than here. The Classical influence was not very apparent except in the high-waisted pinafore-like dresses with widening and squaring necklines. The silhouette was changing from a slim backward-flowing shape to something much more solid and stiff. Beatrice d'Este, a leader of cultured society, may have been responsible for this. As Duchess of Milan, a state closely connected with Spain, she can be seen in her portraits wearing the styles influenced by that country – the long ribbon-trimmed pigtail and the skirts stiffened over a frame which were to be the high fashion of the sixteenth century. Much more linen was allowed to show over the tops of bodices, at the shoulder and through the gaps in sleeve seams as in the male garments. The gowns now became open down the front but the heavy beauty of the lovely damask material was seen to advantage in the natural and well proportioned line.

Italian women had always disliked covering up their hair and at the end of the century it was very simply treated with lovelocks falling either side of the face from a centre parting with the back hair left in a tress, or plait for young girls, or loosely coiled up for a young matron. Veils were to the older woman what the long gowns were to elderly men, a dignified shelter for less sprightly figures and looks, and they also seem to have worn something rarely seen in medieval pictures – a cloak for outdoor wear.

*Italian High Renaissance Dress, 1490*

PLATE XX

# Franco-Flemish Transitional Dress

## Late 15th century

Italy was not destined to enjoy her peace, prosperity and prestige into the sixteenth century. She had been the gnawing envy of her neighbours for many years and only the fact that they were otherwise offensively engaged against each other had spared her for so long. Germany, Burgundy and France had all been her customers and absorbed her goods and some of her polished behaviour but a share in her wealth was what they all hankered after, especially France who had developed big ideas after her wonderful recovery from economic and cultural depths caused by the Hundred Years War and constant occupation by English soldiers.

Although the most persistent contender for European power, Charles the Bold of Burgundy, had been removed permanently from the scene in 1476, other personalities had arisen to challenge France's claim to leadership: Maximilian of Austria (Charles' son-in-law and inheritor through his wife of all the treasures of the Netherlands), Henry VII of England, and a new menace in the Portuguese and Spanish kings. Prestige costs money and no nation has held it long without that useful commodity, even if borrowed or stolen, and Italy was ripe for plundering. With the excuse of a dynastic claim to the throne of Naples, Charles VIII struck, and as the male population had now become what Machiavelli despisingly termed 'soft, with no valour or discipline', the French had an unopposed military tour right through Italy.

The Italians were overawed by the magnificent French army but the invaders too had an eye-opener in the highest standard of living they had ever experienced and all the glorious luxuries that made up the good life – to which they helped themselves or spoilt for the enjoyment of others. This was just the first of many such barbaric invasions and Italy gradually sank under the blows from her greedy enemies; but her industries survived to produce the goods, armour, silks, pottery and gold-work demanded by her triumphant conquerors, but in diminishing good taste as that of the customers predominated.

Good taste is innate – anyone may have it – unlike the special looks of the aristocracy which come by interbreeding between people of perhaps physical comeliness and the means to ensure a care of the body as well as a superiority that comes from giving orders. Both these requirements for distinction the new nations lacked. One can see the difference in the looks of the Italian donors (of good family) of the Portinari altarpiece painted by a Flemish artist compared with local donors in other works; and when it comes to good taste, most of the aspiring nations were as yet untutored and had a childish leaning towards glitter and ostentation. France, of course, had a very old tradition of culture which had been centred on Paris; the rest of the country had been so isolated by war that it was as if the nation as a whole was starting afresh. Italy lost its social lead in European affairs but its influence had lasted for so long and the interchange of merchants had been so frequent that other nations continued to follow its ways and certainly its fashions. The rude, mercenary soldiers from Switzerland were the first to take up Italian styles in a big way and, adapting them to their own characteristics, changed the whole appearance of people at the turn of the century. The mercenaries were employed by many of the Italian states, by Maximilian as his standing army, and were the striking force of the French army (making military strategy extremely difficult when they found themselves on opposing sides). They had already enjoyed the spoils (glorious silks and tapestries) of their victory over Charles the Bold and his Burgundian knights and had exaggerated the fashion for slits and puffs, but the original style was that devised by Italy in the 1480s. The French, who had followed the angular Burgundian fashion, took longer to adapt themselves to the new wider silhouette but by 1490 their appearance takes on a very noticeable change while still retaining some medieval features.

Fashion was to make the individual appear to grow up in the sixteenth century and these *fin-de-siècle* styles seem to be the last wild extravagance of youthful fancy-dress before becoming soberly adult. The women changed more quickly than the men with their heavy dresses, much plainer and cut higher in the neck showing a tucker of white chemise over the square or convex neckline or with the bodice laced across a wide plaston front. The skirts were often lifted and fastened up at the back in bourgeois style showing a contrasting-coloured kirtle. Sleeves were long, projecting over the hands with puffs of chemise showing at the open seams at elbow and down the forearm, or were beginning to widen like bishops' sleeves.

The head-dresses made the greatest change in the appearance of women. Where the hair had been uncovered or tall caps had perched, the head was now enveloped in prim and concealing bonnets and hoods. Anne of Brittany, the pious wife of two French kings, was probably responsible for the flattened hoods worn in France, the Netherlands and England which, in accordance with the wider line of fashion, discarded the gay *hennins* they had supported and now lay like dark bands flat over the head and as lappets on to the shoulders. The turban bonnets were more a German–Swiss style – wired or stuffed, they rose from a band into a halo or tammy shape, often latticed with gold thread and beads. Unmarried girls wore their hair loose down the back by the whole effect was primmer and more matronly. After years of the bald look, a little hair was allowed to show at the sides and was parted neatly and drawn back under the hoods. The white wimples and hoods of working women were so concealing as to be like nun's veils – which indeed is what they became.

The men of the transitional period seem more reluctant to grow up, with their short doublets and long parti-coloured legs. The main change in their fashion was in the width which relied on a loose fit and wide lapels to give the fashionable line so different from the previous Burgundian style of padding on chest and shoulders to emphasize a small waist. Doublets were scooped out in front to fasten in a narrow band or basque at the waist, exposing a wide shirt-front of a contrasting colour or an embroidered vest. The Flemish and French retained the higher neckline in contrast to the negligée styles of Germany and Switzerland. Sleeves now had puffed tops joined to close-fitting pieces on the lower arm. The French retained the long, hanging sleeves on jackets and jerkins, slit up the seam for the arm to come through, but the jacket was now wide with a flat collar and revers of fur. Where in Italy young and old were wearing small caps the French exaggerated the old style of huge beaver hats (swathed in scarves and trimmed with large upstanding feathers) which they often slung on their backs, in the manner of the old *chaperon*, by fancy scarves. Shoes underwent a great change by losing their long points and becoming wide and blunted with low backs.

As contact between countries became easier a more universal fashion prevailed with the influence always from the most successful and powerful nation. Then, there were other means of seeing current fashion with the new method of printing pictures from wood cuts, especially the playing cards which showed many costumes of all and sundry conditions of men. After Venice they were produced mainly in Germany and so influenced the swing of fashion to the north which we describe in Volume III of this History.

*Franco-Flemish Court Dress, 1480*